TAKING IN STUDENTS

GW00493223

A selection of other Family Reference titles in this Series

Arranging Insurance
Be a Local Councillor
Be an Effective School Governor
Becoming a Father
Buying a Personal Computer
Cash from Your Computer
Choose a Private School
Choosing a Nursing Home
Choosing a Package Holiday
Claim State Benefits
Dealing with a Death in the Family
Helping Your Child to Read
Lose Weight and Keep Fit
Making a Complaint
Making a Video
Make a Wedding Speech
Managing Your Personal Finances
Plan a Wedding
Prepare Your Child for School
Raise Funds and Sponsorship
Run a Local Campaign
Run a Voluntary Group
Successful Grandparenting
Successful Single Parenting
Survive Divorce
Take Care of Your Heart
Winning Consumer Competitions

Other titles in preparation

The How To series now contains more than 150 titles in the following categories:

Business Basics
Family Reference
Jobs and Careers
Living and Working Abroad
Student Handbooks
Successful Writing

Please send for a free copy of the latest catalogue for full details (see back cover for address).

FAMILY REFERENCE

TAKING IN STUDENTS

How to make your spare room pay

Rosemary Bartholomew

YOU'RE HOMESICK, AREN'T YOU?

How To Books

Cartoons by Mike Flanagan

British Library Cataloguing in Publication Data
A catalogue record for this book is available from the British Library.

First published in 1996 by How To Books Ltd, Plymbridge House, Estover Road, Plymouth PL6 7PZ, United Kingdom.
Tel: (01752) 202301. Fax: (01752) 202331.

Note: The material contained in this book is set out in good faith for general guidance and no liability can be accepted for loss or expense incurred as a result of relying in particular circumstances on statements made in the book. The laws and regulations are complex and liable to change, and readers should check the current position with the relevant authorities before making personal arrangements.

Produced for How To Books by Deer Park Productions.
Typeset by PDQ Typesetting, Stoke-on-Trent, Staffs.
Printed and bound by Cromwell Press, Broughton Gifford, Melksham, Wiltshire.

Contents

List of illustrations

8

Preface

Every year hundreds of thousands of young people leave home for the first time to eagerly embark on their chosen course of study. Ahead of them is a whole new way of life, full of wide-ranging opportunities and many new experiences.

All of these students, whether they are from universities, colleges of further education, training centres or language schools, need somewhere to live. Although a number will be accommodated on campus, or make their own self-catering arrangements, many will take rooms in private family homes and live as one of the family. This is particularly so for the ever-increasing numbers of students from overseas.

The aim of this book is to explore the issues involved in taking a student into your home. It will show you realistically what to expect, looking at the practicalities, problems and benefits.

THANKS AND ACKNOWLEDGEMENTS

I am grateful to many people, without whose help I could not have written this book. In particular I would like to thank:

Christine Hall, who suggested in the first place I try writing this book and gave me the much-needed push to get started.

Christian Senyk, from Sweden, the first student I ever had to stay fifteen years ago and who immediately became like one of the family.

Christian's mother, Gunilla, now a close friend, who helped by gathering comments from students for me.

Amaia Prieto, from Spain, the student staying with me while this book was being written, who spent much time discussing it with me and also helped by getting her friends to complete my questionnaire.

David Watson, Joyce Cox, Marjorie and Michael Smith for their unfailing support and encouragement.

Nick Hill, who came to stay for six months five years ago and never left, for often cooking the dinner so that I could carry on writing.

Oksana Higglesden from ARELS, and Maureen Peirce from BASELT, for their help and permission to reproduce the ARELS/BASELT Homestay Code of Practice.

The British Council for permission to reproduce details of their student's room requirements.

Sussex Police, East Sussex Fire Service and Hastings Borough Council for providing me with useful information and leaflets.

Dee Fry and other accommodation officers from universities, colleges and language schools for their help in providing background information and answering my many questions.

Most importantly, but too numerous to mention individually, all the students, landladies and host families who spent time talking to me about their experiences and gave me much of the material for this book.

Lastly, but by no means least, my family: my sisters Edna Smith and Lesley Carver, who have always been supportive of my writing aspirations, and my very special thanks to my son, Richard, who gave me the practical means to write this book by letting me use both his brand-new computer and his room as a study whilst he was away teaching students in Japan, and who never doubted my ability to get this book finished!

Rosemary Bartholomew

1
Thinking it Over

NEEDING SOME EXTRA INCOME

Living can be an expensive business. Very few of us are fortunate enough not to have cash flow problems from time to time or even *all* the time. There are so many demands on our money that managing it effectively can be an on-going struggle. Paying for basic essentials such as food, mortgage or rent, household expenses and so on often means that little, or nothing, is left for holidays, new clothes, hobbies and other extras we like to enjoy.

Whatever you need it for, additional income is always welcome and useful. Using your spare room to take in students is one way of increasing your cash flow and well worth trying.

DISCUSSING THE IDEA

Don't rush into things. Give yourself time to think the idea over in a leisurely way and discuss it fully. There are a number of different options and aspects to weigh up. After all, agreeing to share your home with one or more students is something which needs careful consideration. The arrival of a different person – who you will know very little about to begin with – will take some getting used to. Everyone in the household will be affected to some degree and it is therefore only right that they get the chance to air any opinions when you are making your plans.

Talking to the family
Put the idea to the whole family and talk it through.

- Take everyone's feelings and viewpoints into account.

- Make them all feel they have contributed to the decision.

This makes the idea more appealing than if you simply say 'I've decided we're going to have a student.'

Involving the children
Younger children are very often keen on the idea of someone coming to stay. They have a natural curiosity and the thought of meeting a new person – especially one who may be from a different country – is exciting to them.

It is particularly important to consult fully with any older children and teenagers in the family. They usually have plenty of opinions and views about everything, and it is definitely helpful to get them involved in a positive way at the start to avoid possible jealousies and arguments. The idea may appeal to them but it is also quite possible they will decide to express strong objections. Often they will come round if you explain the benefits to the family which can be gained. They may benefit not only from the financial boost, but also from getting to know someone else, hopefully making a new friend and, perhaps, if the student is from overseas, learning about another country.

WHAT SORT OF PEOPLE TAKE IN STUDENTS?

The answer, quite simply, is all sorts of people in all kinds of situations.

You can be:

Single	Living with a partner
Married	With or without children
Divorced	In employment or unemployed
Widowed	Retired

You can live in:

A flat	A bungalow
A terraced house	A detached house
A semi-detached house	Your own property
Rented accommodation	

Fig. 1. What sort of people take in students?

Consulting with your partner

The support of your partner is essential if the project is to be successful. However, once having been persuaded that the idea is worth trying, the vast majority are usually not over-concerned about the options and practicalities so long as there is not too much disruption to their lifestyle!

Deciding on your own

If you live on your own then you have nobody else's views to consider. You can decide just what is best for you.

However, it could be argued that a single person's home is where the presence of someone else would have a greater effect. In a busy family household of several people one more might not make such a great deal of difference. If you are used to your own company and the freedom to do things to suit yourself then be prepared to adapt to changes.

Listening to the advice of friends or colleagues

When thinking about taking in a student it is a good idea to talk to other people who have already tried it. You may have a relative, friend, or know someone at work who would be more than happy to recount how things worked out for them. Learning from the first-hand experiences of others can often be very useful.

DECIDING WHAT YOU COULD OFFER A STUDENT

Take some time to consider exactly what you could offer a student, and what you would be able to provide easily. The following list can be used as a guide.

- Do you have a comfortable room available, equipped with a desk for studying?

- Can you offer accommodation for just a few weeks or all the year round?

- Are you prepared to offer **full board, half board, bed and breakfast** or just a room?

- Are you able to be flexible about mealtimes?

- Could you provide for special dietary needs or preferences such as vegetarian?

- Would you be happy for the student to use your kitchen to cook his/her own meals?

- Are you prepared to offer a laundry service or use of your facilities?

- Are you willing to provide a regular cleaning service?

- Are you able to ensure privacy, peace and quiet for studying?

- Would you treat your student as one of the family and have an interest in their welfare?

- Would you have time to help your student with any problems?

- Could you offer help with English to a foreign student?

- Would you be prepared to take in a student with disabilities?

- Could you take a student at very short notice?

You do not have to offer all these things, but you do need to think carefully about which ones you can, and want to, offer. Different organisations and students have different requirements. What is on offer and what is required need to match up. Not all types of student will be right for your particular circumstances and vice versa.

CONSIDERING DIFFERENT OPTIONS

- What sort of student are you going to look for?

- What different options are available?

Start by listing the possibilities in your area.

Looking at local establishments

First you need to check what sort of organisations there are within easy travelling distance of your home which might want accommodation for students. These could be:

1. Universities.

2. Colleges of further education.

3.   Language schools.

4.   Vocational training colleges and schools, such as:

     teacher training colleges
     agricultural colleges
     schools or institutes of nursing
     business training centres.

5.   Conference/residential centres which may run seminars or leisure courses.

Some starting points
- Wherever there are students, there is likely to be a need for accommodation.

- On-site residential facilities are often limited and most organisations rely on extra private accommodation for their students.

- Many students have their own transport and are willing to travel several miles daily.

Short-term or long-term accommodation?
Accommodation could be needed for anything from an odd week to a couple of years. The most commonly required periods are

- a complete academic term or year for a university or college student

- or three to four weeks for a summer language school student.

What suits your particular circumstances?
You can sometimes combine both options by having a number of short-term students for a long period, rather than one all the time.

Advantages of offering short-term accommodation
1.   It will cause minimum disruption to your way of life.

2.   The room will be free for other use the rest of the time.

3.   The weekly rate is often higher.

Disadvantages of offering short-term accommodation
1. Changes of student mean more upheaval for the household.

2. You do not have the benefit of extra income for so long.

3. There is not so much time to build up good relationships.

Advantages of offering long-term accommodation
1. You can count on a regular income for longer.

2. You have more time to forge a friendship with your student.

3. Full use is being made of your room.

Disadvantages of offering long-term accommodation
1. There could be a problem if you want to go away.

2. If things don't work out there's a longer period to worry about.

3. The room is not available for other visitors, such as friends and relatives, to use.

Considering teenage or mature students
Although you might rightly imagine most students to be in their late teens or twenties, this is not always the case. Language schools frequently have students aged from 12 or 13, and sometimes even younger, and all establishments have a number of mature students from their twenties to sixties and more. What age would you prefer?

Points to bear in mind
• If you have children of your own, younger teenagers may fit in best.

• You will feel some responsibility for looking after younger ones.

• Teenagers are often happy to share a bedroom.

• Mature adult students will expect little or no restriction on their lifestyle but will hopefully be more responsible!

Choosing which sex
You have the opportunity to specify male, female or no preference. This is entirely up to you and what you feel happiest with.

If you have a teenager in the family, and take in a student of the opposite sex, be sure you can cope with any resultant crushes or declarations of true love. It happens all the time!

Deciding on one, two or more
This depends on how much room you have and how many you feel you can cope with. Some students, particularly younger ones, are happy to share a room. Others want to be on their own.

- The rate per person for a single room is more than for a shared room.

- Having two students will give you a bigger profit margin.

There are people who have several students at the same time and regard this as a home business. This may be fine if you have a large house, can offer adequate facilities and can cope with what is involved. However, remember that reputable organisations will want to be sure that there is no over-crowding. Also remember that with younger language school students they come here to experience normal British family life.

Choosing different nationalities
If you are having a student from overseas you may be able to express a preference for certain nationalities. This can be helpful if someone in the family is studying a language and wants the chance to practise their conversation skills with a native of the relevant country. Or you may have an interest in visiting a country and want to learn more about it. On the other hand you may have no preference and be happy to take whoever is allocated to you.

Some non-European students are more difficult to place because they come from countries with completely different customs and dietary requirements, which families may not feel happy about. Often enhanced payments may be offered for these students because of any extra inconvenience involved.

Helping disabled students
Sometimes there is a shortage of accommodation for students with certain disabilities, for example those in wheelchairs who might need some special residential facilities not available at the college or school. If you have a bungalow, or ground-floor room with facilities, and can be around to lend a hand when required, this can be of

great help. Usually these students are fiercely determined to lead as normal a life as possible and will not want to be fussed over, but there is great satisfaction to be gained from helping to make it possible for these students to carry on with their studies.

Being on stand-by
Many organisations like to have a list of people to take in students on an emergency basis. This could happen when:

(a) There is a sudden illness or trauma where a student is living and he/she needs to be moved.

(b) The placement is not working out.

(c) The offer of accommodation is withdrawn at the last moment.

This could involve taking in a student at very short notice, perhaps immediately. If you are able to do this then you are likely to be welcomed with open arms by **Accommodation Officers**. Sometimes people with two spare rooms keep the second for such emergencies. Other people are happy to be on **emergency stand-by** only and they are often approached regularly.

Providing accommodation with tuition
A small number of specialised language schools look for families where students can be placed in the home of a suitably qualified person – such as someone with a **TEFL** (Teaching English as a Foreign Language) certificate, or a degree – where they can be given tuition on a one-to-one basis whilst living as one of the family. These placements attract an appropriate fee in recognition of the services provided but the selection requirements are high.

Keeping your options open
The more flexible you can be, the more students will be available to you. If you have too many restrictions you could find your room stays empty for longer.

Very many people decide to start with a student for just one summer, or term, and then if the experience proves rewarding they do it each year or all year.

So having decided which options seem available and suitable (see Figure 2), let us now look more fully at what exactly would be expected.

LOOKING AT DIFFERENT REQUIREMENTS

Needs vary from establishment to establishment and from student to student.

- Some want just a room, with use of cooking and other facilities.

- Others want bed and breakfast, half board or full board.

- There are students who want to feel part of the family and those who want to live as independently as possible.

Registered organisations will generally issue you with some sort of guidelines so that you know exactly what is expected.

Providing a room only

Your student will probably eat out for most of the time at college or university. However, you will need to provide access to cooking facilities at agreed times and somewhere for the student's food to be kept. Access to bathroom facilities needs to be available and use of laundry facilities is appreciated.

You will need to decide on arrangements for room cleaning. You may want to do it yourself on a weekly basis or you may expect it to be done by the student. Usually you will provide pillows and blankets, and stipulate that the student brings his or her own bed linen and towels.

Providing room and part or full board

You can offer to provide just breakfast, half or full board. You could decide that this will be flexible, for example bed and breakfast but with additional meals by arrangement when required.

You will need to provide bathroom facilities and, usually, either a laundry service or use of laundry facilities. You will be responsible for room cleaning and for providing towels and bed linen unless otherwise agreed.

Providing host family or homestay accommodation

Host families are expected to do more than just provide board and lodgings. Students needing this kind of accommodation expect to live as one of the family and to share in family life. Many are under 16 and you will therefore undertake some responsibility for their welfare.

What kind of student?
University student
College student
Language school student
Vocational student
Leisure course student

Long- or short-term accommodation?
One or several weeks, one term or one year?

What age?
Younger teenage or mature student?

What sex?
Male, female or no preference?

How many?
One, two or more?

What nationality?
Want to practise your French or German?

Could you take in a disabled student?
Is your home wheelchair-friendly?

What about being on stand-by?
Could you take someone in at half-an-hour's notice?

Could you provide accommodation with tuition?
Do you have any teaching skills?

What requirements can you meet?
Room only
Room and board
Host family

Have you decided on your preferred options?

Fig. 2. Your options at a glance.

Reputable schools will ensure that your home is inspected and they will also want to know details about the family. This is covered in depth in Chapter 3.

QUESTIONS AND ANSWERS

What do you think are the main qualities needed in a person planning to take in students?

Without doubt you need a sense of humour. You also need to have an interest in people, some flexibility and a positive approach. Diplomacy skills are also useful, as are patience and a certain amount of tolerance.

How can I be sure that everything will work out well with no problems?

The short answer is – you can't! You do need to be realistic and accept that things could go wrong in some cases. This book aims to show you how to gain the most from your 'studenting' experience, keep any problems to a minimum and deal with any that do arise. It is, however, important not to create any problems yourself by negative thinking and to realise that the majority of students fit in well and happily.

CHECKLIST

• Talk over the idea with as many people as possible.

• Gain the support of your family and listen to their views.

• Consider the different options open to you.

• Decide just what type of board and accommodation you are prepared to offer.

• Work out precisely what your commitment would be.

CASE STUDIES

Let's now meet a variety of people who are deciding to go ahead with taking in students. We will be following their experiences in the succeeding chapters, seeing how they get on, how they cope with any problems or difficulties and what benefits they gain.

Angela and Tony want to stretch the family budget

Angela and Tony Marshall, a married couple with two children, are in their early thirties. They have a four-year-old son and a daughter of eighteen months. Tony works for a printing firm and they live in an older-style, three-bedroomed terraced house which they are gradually improving with the help of a friend.

Since Angela gave up work to have the children, making the money stretch has become difficult. While the children are young they can share a bedroom which means that at present the third bedroom could be used for students.

There are several language schools nearby which advertise in the summer months for host families. As the room is large enough, Angela and Tony decide to apply for two teenage students.

Claire wants help with the expenses

Claire Reed is 27, single, works full-time in a bank and is aiming for promotion. Her live-in boyfriend has recently left and Claire is now struggling to meet the payments on her two-bedroomed flat alone. She needs someone to move into the second bedroom and help with the expenses.

Claire is too busy to spend time looking after anyone. She wants someone who would do her own cooking, share the housework and not get in her way too much. There is a hospital nearby with a school of nursing attached. She thinks a student nurse might be a possibility.

Helen considers taking in a university student

Helen Darrell, a divorcee in her mid-forties, works part-time as a sales assistant in a department store. She lives in a three-bedroomed, semi-detached house with her daughter Debbie who is 16 and still at school. Her son left home nearly a year ago to live with his girlfriend and since then his room has only been used for occasional guests.

Helen is finding that, on a part-time income and with a teenager to support, money is tight and does not allow for such things as the holidays abroad which she would like. She does not want to have a full-time job and so thinks that having a student from the nearby university might be the answer. She is also hopeful this might encourage Debbie to study harder.

Barbara looks for companionship as well as income

Barbara Chandler, a widow, lives in a two-bedroomed bungalow with just her dog for company. She has recently been made redundant because the firm where she worked has closed down. However, she feels that being in her fifties she is not at the right age to start looking for another job and would be unlikely to find anything. She misses the companionship of her work colleagues and feels a little extra income would be useful to supplement her occupational pension. Taking in a student would help on both counts by giving her someone to take an interest in and boosting her finances. She is considering opting for a lady student from a local teacher training college.

DISCUSSION POINTS

1. What benefits would there be for you from having a student?

2. How much or how little involved would you want to be?

3. How easily would you adapt to a student sharing your home?

2
Preparing the Room

Before you go ahead with actively finding your student you need to make sure that the room is in a satisfactory condition and contains all that will be needed.
The main requirements you need to consider are:

1. A good state of repair and decoration.
2. Providing a comfortable bed.
3. Arranging an area and facilities for study.
4. Providing sufficient storage space for clothes.
5. Ensuring adequate heating and lighting.

LOOKING AT WHAT NEEDS DOING

The room should be clean, comfortable and welcoming. Maybe it already is, in which case you have no worries. On the other hand, it may not have been used for a long time and look neglected. It could have peeling wallpaper and grubby paintwork, or be full of accumulated junk. If so, you need to get on with putting it to rights.
First take a good, critical look at the room and decide:

- Does it need any major preparation work, such as damp patches dealt with or replastering?

- Does it want complete redecoration or just a freshen up?

- Do you need any shelves put up?

- Are there adequate electricity sockets?

- Is it worth installing a washbasin?

- Are you able to carry out the necessary work yourself?

- Are you going to need professional help?

- Will you need any new furniture?

- How much can you realistically afford to spend?

Once you have decided what needs doing – it's time for action!

Clearing out

Before you start work, clear out everything that won't be needed. If you are one of those people who has a collection of items that 'might be useful one day' in your spare room, now is the time to sort them out. Be ruthless. You need to either find a new place to store them or else get rid of them.

If you haven't used something for six months, and are never likely to, you would be better off with cash in your pocket from selling it. Why not consider loading up all the unwanted items and going to a car boot sale? It's surprising what you can get rid of that way and this will help towards the decorating or furnishing costs. Or you could donate them to your local charity shop.

Once the room is clear, work can start.

Getting professional help

If there is necessary work which you are unable to carry out yourself, you need to engage a reliable and competent person to do it for you.

Asking for recommendations

Ask friends, neighbours or people at work if they have used a particular firm or person; satisfied previous customers are always the best recommendation.

It is worth keeping an eye out for a retired professional who still likes to keep his hand in with the occasional job. He has the benefit of years of experience but is likely to offer you a much cheaper quote than a firm would.

Obtaining quotes

Quotes can differ widely so it is wise to get about three. Take into consideration not just the price, but the way in which your request for a quote is handled:

- Does the tradesman turn up at the agreed time to look at the work?

- Is he business-like and courteous?

- Does he ask detailed questions about what you want and make notes?

- Is he in a hurry, taking thirty seconds to give you a price?

- Does he try to persuade you to have additional work done?

- Does he seem to know what he is talking about and give you a feeling of confidence that the job would be completed to your satisfaction?

- How long would the work take and when could it be done?

After considering all these points, choose the one you feel would give the best value for money. This is often not the cheapest nor the dearest!

Doing it yourself

You will, of course, save a lot of money by doing as much as possible yourself. So although you may need a builder to fix the damp patch, or an electrician to put in an extra socket, perhaps you could have a go at any decorating yourself.

It may be that you only need to freshen up the room with a new coat of paint. It is worth investing in good quality paint brushes; sometimes with cheaper ones you will find hairs left in your paint-work.

If you decide to wallpaper there is a wide variety to suit every pocket. An inexpensive and popular choice is wood-chip paper, which is then simply emulsioned over. This has the advantage of being easy to hang, even for complete beginners, and there is no pattern-matching to worry about. In future years all you need do is re-emulsion for a fresh look.

Look for closing-down or other sales when wallpaper and paint prices are slashed drastically.

Deciding on a colour scheme

This is largely a matter of personal preference, and any decorating shop has free colour chart leaflets and trial-size pots of paint. Remember light colours or small patterns will make the room seem bigger, and pastel shades are more relaxing. You may consider that a neutral shade, such as magnolia, would be the best option.

- A point to remember when decorating the room is that the majority of students, especially long-stay ones, will like to make the room feel like home by putting up their own posters around the walls.

PROVIDING A STUDY AREA

Your student's room will need to be a combined bedroom and study. It is essential to provide a desk, or at least a table, to work at. Obviously a desk, with drawer space for papers and books, is preferable. If you don't already have one, look around the second-hand shops or in your local paper's For Sale section. Desks are usually easy to find at a reasonable price. Students have been known to complain that this most basic requirement is not provided and that they are expected to work at the dining room table! Whilst this might do for short-term holiday students, who perhaps have little written work to complete, it is not acceptable for examination students who need to be able to study in privacy and quiet, without interruption.

- Bear in mind that, especially with university and college students, it is quite possible he or she will want to bring a computer to use. Make sure the desk is positioned near the electricity sockets.

- A comfortable chair of the right height is also important.

- Useful optional extras are a small bookcase or shelf near the desk, and a noticeboard for timetable and notices to be pinned up.

OTHER FURNITURE AND FURNISHINGS

It is not necessary to go to a great deal of expense. Good items can be picked up secondhand, and you should watch the sales for cut-price offers on things like towels and linen. Plan what you need carefully and shop around. It's a good idea to make a list so that nothing is forgotten.

Choosing the furniture

Bed
Test for comfort and soundness by trying it out yourself. Check the mattress; it's wise to invest in a cover to protect it. If you are short of storage space a bed with built-in drawers is worth thinking about.

Wardrobe
For maximum storage choose one with a shelf and/or drawer. If room space is limited, look for one with sliding doors.

Chest of drawers
This can double up as a dressing table. You may decide a small one is adequate for summer visitors but bear in mind that long-stay guests will have more clothes to store.

Bedside cabinet
Optional; if the chest of drawers is placed next to the bed you probably won't need one.

Easy chair
Optional and dependent on amount of room.

Small coffee/occasional table
This would be useful to have beside the easy chair or bed.

Shelving
A couple of shelves, perhaps across an alcove, will be very useful for books and/or tapes, CDs and knick-knacks.

Bookcase
Optional and probably not needed if you have shelving.

Good planning
Plan the room to give as much space as possible and avoid over-crowding. Try moving the furniture into several different positions to see what looks best.

Furnishings

- Take a good look at the carpet: it is satisfactory or would it benefit from being cleaned?

• What about the curtains? Do you need new ones or will popping them in the washing machine suffice?

• If you are providing bed linen and towels do you have enough to allow for at least two changes?

• Have you got spare pillows and blankets in case they are needed?

DECIDING ON THE FACILITIES

Installing a wash-basin

A very important point to decide is whether to have a wash-basin in the room.

Advantages
1. It will upgrade the room and this can be reflected in your charges.

2. It will give more privacy, and help with the inevitable bathroom queue.

3. A vanity-type unit will give valuable storage space underneath.

Disadvantages
1. It is an expensive outlay.

2. You would additionally need to have a splash-back or tiles above the wash-basin, increasing the outlay.

3. Installing a wash-basin may mean there is not enough space for all the furniture, particularly a second bed if you want two students.

Providing a television

The majority of people enjoy watching television. Although most families will invite the student to share family viewing in the lounge, some also like to provide a separate television. There may be different programmes you want to watch, you may be entertaining friends and want the lounge to yourself. You may want to read or listen to music and not want the television on. You may well be able to find a reasonably priced second-hand or reconditioned model.

If you are having summer students who are likely to be out every evening then you will probably not consider supplying a television.

Providing a radio-alarm

A bedside clock-radio-alarm is a good idea, although not essential. Some students may bring a travel alarm with them. However, most don't and will ask you to either lend them a clock or bang on their door to wake them up!

Electricity sockets

Make sure that there are sufficient for likely requirements and that they can be reached easily without moving furniture.

HEATING AND LIGHTING

Looking at heating options

Your student needs to be warm and comfortable. If you have central heating, radiators with individual temperature controls offer the best choice.

If you do not have central heating, think carefully. Overseas students in particular have no conception of how expensive electricity is in this country. They will think nothing of leaving a heater on while they go out for the day and you will find your bills rise rapidly. Language schools surveys have shown one of the most common complaints from students is that they are not warm enough and that, even where there is central heating, it is not on for long enough. Foreign students are often surprised to find that in many British homes there is no heating on at night and that it is not considered necessary. Often they come from homes which we would consider uncomfortably hot and some adjustment is needed. Make sure there are always extra blankets on hand.

- Gas fires and anything with a flame must be ruled out for safety reasons in bedrooms.

- Electric bar fires are very expensive to run and are also a hazard in a student's room.

- Oil-filled electric radiators, which can be purchased with temperature controls and time settings, are one of the most economical and safe options.

Your local electricity showroom staff will be pleased to advise you on running costs of different heaters.

Providing adequate lighting

Ideally there should be available a choice of both a good, strong main light and also more subdued lighting for relaxation.

* A bedside lamp is useful and can be picked up for a few pounds.
* You may also need a flexible desk-lamp to ensure adequate lighting in the study area.

ADDING FINISHING TOUCHES

Don't forget the small but important additions such as:

* a mirror
* waste-paper bin
* coat-hangers.

An extra hook on the back of the door is always extremely useful. A linen bin may also be useful, but not essential.

It is not wise, or necessary, to have a lot of ornaments in the room. They will probably be pushed aside to make room for all the clutter necessary to student life!

If the room looks bare, think about putting something on the wall – perhaps a poster or two – for short-stay students. Long-term students will usually bring their own bits and pieces.

First impressions are important. If the room looks welcoming and comfortable, and your student can see you have gone to a little trouble, it will help get the relationship off to a good start.

QUESTIONS AND ANSWERS

Many people say that it is not worth providing anything of good quality for students since they will probably not appreciate it or take care of it. Is this true?

To a certain extent, yes! However, whilst you are not expected to provide expensive, top-quality items, adequate basic standards of comfort must be ensured. After all, you are being paid to provide this. No student, or anyone else for that matter, would be happy to have an old, rickety bed with an uncomfortable lumpy mattress. They have a right to expect better. You also need to remember that there are some mature students, such as business executives, who will pay a higher fee and will therefore be entitled to expect an accordingly higher standard of accommodation and comfort.

Clear the room out

Take unwanted items to charity shop or car boot sale

Arrange for any quotes needed eg installing wash-basin,
putting in additional electricity socket

Choose which quotes to go ahead with and confirm

Buy decorating requirements if needed

Take curtains down and wash them

Get all necessary work done - whether by workmen,
friends or yourself

Clean inside of windows and put fresh curtains up

Get carpet cleaned

Decide on the furniture needed

Look in sales, second-hand shop or newspaper adverts
for any items needed

Arrange (and re-arrange!) the furniture

Obtain the small items such as waste-paper bin, lamp
and other necessities

Shop around for bedding, linen and towels

Make the bed up ready

Check for anything which may have been overlooked

Give a final dust and polish to the room

It's ready for your student!

Fig. 3. Action plan.

We do not have a permanent spare room but plan to move our two children in together so one of their rooms can be used. Is this acceptable?

Yes. In fact many families do this, especially for short-term summer students. However, do explain things to your child and make sure that all their possessions are moved too. They will need to understand they cannot go in and out of the room when someone else is staying in it.

We plan to have two teenage students. Can we put them in bunk beds?

The answer to this is probably no. Most accommodation requirements will specify that bunk beds are definitely not acceptable. However – providing they are full-length and not child-size – it's possible to get round this if you have room to separate them and use them as twin beds.

CHECKLIST

• Decide what needs doing in the room.

• If you need professional decorating help, get quotes.

• Clear out any unwanted items and try selling them.

• Consider the room's facilities, furniture and furnishings.

• Make sure you have safe and efficient heating.

◗ Give a choice of bright and soft lighting.

• Remember the small things like waste-paper bin and coat hangers.

• Add your own finishing touches to make it welcoming.

CASE STUDIES

Angela and Tony try DIY

Angela and Tony have not yet got around to decorating their spare room as they haven't needed to use it. It is in a pretty poor state with shabby, peeling wallpaper and dingy-looking paint. It needs

Angela's Shopping List

DIY Shop

Woodchip paper
Wallpaper paste
White matt emulsion (for ceiling)
Magnolia matt emulsion (for walls)
White gloss paint (for woodwork)

Furniture shop

Twin beds

Second-hand shop

Double wardrobe
Chest of drawers (big enough for 2 to share)
Table
Two chairs

Market / Department Store

2 duvets

4 pillows

4 duvet and pillow cover sets

4 fitted bottom sheets

2 mattress covers

4 bath towels

6 hand towels

2 blankets

Ready made curtains

Waste-paper bins

Fig. 4. Shopping list.

complete redecoration but they cannot afford to have it done professionally. So far they have done all the decorating in their house themselves, with the help of a friend for any difficult bits.

They need to strip all the old paper off before they can start. Angela works at this when she can during the day, while her son is at playgroup and her mother looks after her younger child. Tony then helps in the evening and at weekends. They choose wood-chip paper and emulsion as this is an economical option. Angela then plans to have a couple of posters on the walls to brighten the room.

Central heating is something they hope to put in sometime. For now they use electric plug-in radiators.

Angela buys new twin beds in the lower price range, but gets the rest of the furniture second-hand at reasonable prices. She looks in the local market for furnishing bargains.

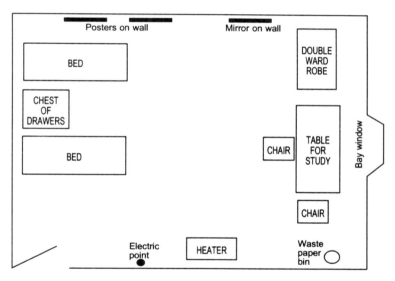

1. Angela and Tony have a room sufficiently spacious for two students. It will also allow for alternative furniture arrangements if desired

2. The wardrobe is a double one and the chest of drawers has four drawers to allow two per student.

3. A large table has been provided instead of a smaller desk. This is a good idea since two students may be using it at the same time.

Fig. 5. Angela and Tony's room layout.

Claire decides to leave things as they are

Claire has decided that whoever moves into the room can take it as they find it. Although the paper is peeling in places she reckons that this could be covered with posters. The flat does not have central heating and at the moment there is no heating of any kind in the room.

The room is furnished with a single bed, second-hand wardrobe and chest of drawers only. There is not enough space for a desk. Claire doesn't feel it necessary to go to a lot of expense because she knows that accommodation is in heavy demand in her area and students are grateful to find anything.

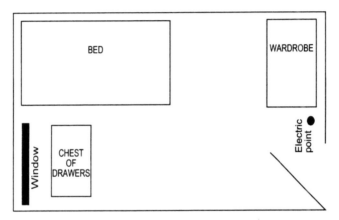

1. The small size of Claire's room is limiting and the addition of a desk would make it overcrowded.

2. Space-saving ideas would help make better use of the room:
   (a) A bed with built-in drawers underneath would provide more storage space.
   (b) So would a taller wardrobe with an additional shelf and drawer. If these were provided, the chest of drawers could be exchanged for a desk.
   (c) Alternatively, fixing a drop-down work surface to the free wall could be considered.

3. Some form of heating needs to be provided in the room. There is only one electricity socket and not much space by it, so it would need to be something very small.

Fig. 6. Claire's room layout.

Helen has a spring-clean

Helen decides that the room is in a reasonable condition and she can manage without having it redecorated. She would like to install a hand-basin because even just she and Debbie often want to use the bathroom at the same time and one more person would make the situation worse. However, because of the cost she feels that this is something which will have to wait until later. So for the moment she just gives the room a thorough spring-clean, washing all the paint-work down, having the carpet shampooed and putting up a pair of fresh curtains. As the room was fully furnished for her son, and is in good condition, she doesn't need to buy anything additional.

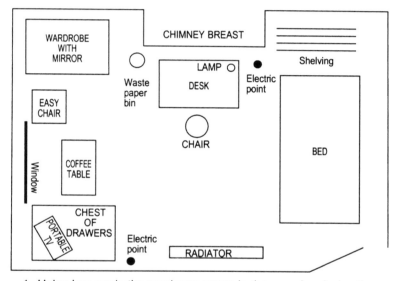

1. Helen has made the maximum space in the room by placing the bed sideways against the wall.

2. The desk was not placed in front of the window because:
   (a) It needs to be positioned near an electricity socket for possible computer use.
   (b) When the window is open papers could get blown about.
   (c) There would be no added distraction caused by looking out of the window instead of studying!

3. The useful shelving in the alcove provides ample storage space for books, tapes and CDs.

Fig. 7. Helen's room layout.

Barbara goes for a total new look

Barbara has decided to use some of her redundancy money to have the room done out professionally. She has a wash-basin installed and the room completely redecorated by a small local firm recommended to her.

As she has decided to have ladies only she can plan a pretty, feminine look. She goes for pinks and florals. She has matching curtains and duvet covers, buying two covers the same so that the look remains coordinated when one cover is in the wash. Barbara also goes for new furniture, buying a wardrobe and two matching chests of drawers. She provides a spacious desk which is positioned by the window for maximum light. She also has a comfortable armchair, coffee table and a colour television in the room.

There is a bowl of pot-pourri, a dried flower arrangement and a couple of china figures to make the room attractive and inviting.

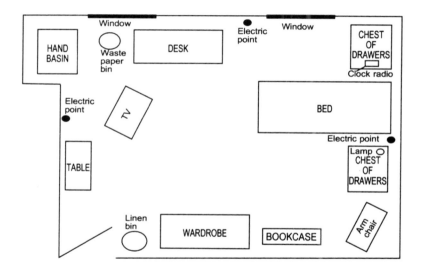

1. Barbara has had a hand-basin installed in the alcove, which immediately upgrades the room.

2. She has plenty of electricity sockets. This gives her maximum alternative choices in rearranging the furniture.

3. She has thoughtfully provided a linen bin.

Fig. 8. Barbara's room layout.

DISCUSSION POINTS

1. What are your long-term plans for the room?

2. How much time and money, if any, are you prepared to invest in improving the room?

3. Imagine yourself as a guest. Would *you* be comfortable living in your spare room?

3
Finding Your Student

Now you are ready to get on with finding your student. You can do this in one of three main ways:

1. Advertise privately.

2. Reply to accommodation wanted advertisements.

3. Telephone establishments direct, on spec.

Additionally, you could try asking friends or acquaintances who already have students. Often they may know whether the organisation they deal with is likely to need more accommodation. Indeed, when demand exceeds supply existing landladies are often asked if they know anyone else who might have a room to offer.

PLACING OR RESPONDING TO ADVERTISEMENTS

There are a number of places where accommodation, both available and wanted, is advertised. These include:

- your local newspaper

- local advertising publications

- shop windows

- notice boards.

Supply and demand varies from area to area. Some areas never have enough accommodation whilst in others it is plentiful.

Advertising privately
Some people, although probably a minority, prefer to find their

student independently and will place their own advertisements.

The advantages of placing your own ad
- You do not have to fill out detailed application or registration forms.

- You avoid paying any possible registration fees.

- You can pick and choose your student more easily.

The disadvantages of placing your own ad
- If there is a problem you cannot expect the establishment your student attends to give you any help.

- There may be limited demand; the majority of students will come from another area and are more likely to apply to the university/ college accommodation office.

- Alternatively, if there is a high demand you may find yourself dealing with dozens of enquiries.

Wording your advertisement
If you do decide that you want to go ahead with an independent advertisement, make sure that it shows:

- Exactly what is on offer, eg half board, full board or self-catering.

- If there are any restrictions, such as females only or non-smokers.

- If there is any particular time for enquirers to ring, eg evenings only.

Consider also including anything which might make your advertisement more appealing. Take a look at the following examples, both placed under the classification Student Accommodation in the local paper.

Example 1
Room and half board available.
Telephone . . .

Example 2
Room and half board available in comfortable and friendly family home near college.
Please telephone . . .

ACCOMMODATION WANTED AND AVAILABLE

Host families

Required for our teenage language students. Three-week courses from June onwards. Full board. Single or shared rooms. Please phone....

Half board

accommodation required for our students.
All year round courses.
Ring now on....

Occasional emergency full/part board accommodation required for our students. Please contact....

Superior half-board accommodation required for our business executive students. Excellent rates. Please contact....

Mature student

Male non-smoker, urgently seeks lodgings near university. Tel....

Our student accommodation register is open now for this year. Please phone for details....

Extra accommodation required due to heavy demand for our popular summer activity courses. Immediate bookings. Phone....

Wanted

By responsible college student: room and use of facilities for one term only. Ring me on....

Room to let

In flat near town centre. Share bills. Female only. Please phone evenings only....

Host families required for our overseas adult students for academic year courses starting in September. Single rooms only. Contact us now....

Can you help?

Ground floor room with breakfast and evening meal required for partly disabled student. Please write to....

Bed, breakfast and evening meal offered in comfortable home. Walking distance from college. References required. Tel....

Fig. 9. Accommodation advertisements.

Although Example 1 is quite adequate and to the point, Example 2 is more detailed and attractive and so is likely to gain more enquiries. Make sure you give your advert a little thought.

Whether or not you indicate your charges is completely up to you. Although it's useful for the student to see at a glance if the price is within his range, many landladies prefer not to divulge this until they receive enquiries.

Deciding where to advertise

Obviously local newspapers and other publications will have the biggest circulation. However, it is well worth initially trying a postcard in a local shop window, or their advertisement board, because:

• This will be much cheaper – pence instead of pounds.

• You pay the same fee however many words you use, so you can provide more details.

• Once you have accepted a student you can remove the card and save being bothered by future callers.

Should you have no success after a week or two then you can try your local paper.

Replying to advertisements

Advertisements placed by organisations

Look carefully at all the advertisements which interest you. At this stage, although you have may decided on the type of student you will try for, you may not have decided on the particular organisation. So if, for example, you intend to apply for a language school student and there are several schools to choose from, consider each one's advertisement. How do they compare? You can obtain details from more than one school and then apply to the one which appeals most. Simply telephone the contact number, mention where you have seen the advertisement, and ask for details and an application form to be sent to you.

Advertisements placed by private individuals

You may be replying to an individual advertisement for accommodation wanted. Before ringing:

Your address
TOWN
Post code

Telephone no.

Date

Name of referee
Address

Dear Mr_____

NAME OF STUDENT (in bold or underlined type)

I am considering providing accommodation in my own home to the above-named whilst he studies at the local college. He has given your name as someone willing to provide a character reference.

I would be grateful if you could please let me know whether you feel he is an honest, trustworthy and reliable person who you think would be a good lodger?

I enclose a stamped addressed envelope for your reply and look forward to hearing from you soon, if possible within the next week.

Thanking you in anticipation of your help.

Yours sincerely

Your signature

[Your name] Mrs or Miss in brackets after

Fig. 10. Example of a reference request.

● Jot down a list of possible questions you might want to ask

● Be prepared to answer questions yourself.

If it sounds as if the person might be a possibility, arrange a convenient time to meet so that the room can be viewed.

Remember, responding to any advertisement only indicates your possible interest. It does not commit you to anything.

Viewing the room

Many landladies do not get the chance to meet their student in advance if they live a distance away or details are arranged by an organisation. If, however, a student does come to view the room then this gives you the advantage of seeing what they are like and giving you the chance to find out a little about them face to face.

Make quite clear what your expectations would be and also be firm about any restrictions. The student will want to know what rules and regulations are going to be imposed and how much freedom allowed. It's important that you both know just where you stand right at the beginning.

Taking up references

If you are going to take an unknown person into your home without the support of an organisation behind you, it is quite likely you may want to take up **references**.

Character references, whilst providing no cast-iron guarantee, are helpful in minimising the chances of taking on someone who is irresponsible or a trouble-maker. Ask for the names of two responsible people who would act as referees. These could be:

● an employer (most students have had a weekend or occasional job)
● a teacher
● an official of any club/organisation the student may belong to
● neighbours
● any previous landlady.

A short, to-the-point letter is all that is needed (see Figure 10). Because it is an 'official' letter typescript looks more business-like, although handwritten may be considered acceptable.

It is important not to forget the stamped addressed envelope. If you need a reply by a certain date you must specify this, otherwise your letter could be put to one side and not dealt with.

STUDENT ACCOMMODATION REGISTRATION FORM

CATEGORY: Room and breakfast

Your name:

Address:

Telephone: Daytime:
                          Evening:

Number of single rooms available:

Number of double/twin rooms available:

Dates of availability from: **to:**

Type of heating:

Will you accept: Males only/Females only   No preference
                         Non-smokers only   Smokers

Do you have: Study facilities in room   Yes/No
                         Wash-basin in room   Yes/No

Laundry: Use of laundry facilities included
                         Extra charge for use of laundry facilities
                         No provision for laundry

Additional meals by arrangement: Yes/No

Use of kitchen: Yes/No

Payment frequency: Weekly/monthly/per term

Rate: Single room
                         Shared room (per person)

Signature:

Date:

Fig. 11. Example of university/college student
accommodation registration form.

CONTACTING ORGANISATIONS ON SPEC

There are some organisations – particularly small ones – which never, or rarely, advertise. 'We hardly ever need to because people ring in constantly,' said one accommodation officer, 'and we find enough places that way.'

It's always worth a try. Look in your local directory and mark off likely establishments in the vicinity. Then ring and simply ask if they need any accommodation for their students and say what you have to offer. There's a good chance if you have rung at the right time that you will be lucky. If not, they may offer to keep your details on file in case they want to contact you later.

COMPLETING APPLICATION AND REGISTRATION FORMS

After replying to an organisation's advertisement you can expect to be sent:

- a covering letter
- details about the organisation itself
- an outline of their accommodation requirements
- terms and conditions
- an application or registration form
- some indication of how quickly you need to return it by.

Read all the information carefully and make sure you have understood it. Then if you think you can meet the requirements and are happy with the terms and conditions, fill out the form.

Looking at some questions you may be asked

If you aim to provide accommodation to a British university or college student you will probably only be asked basic questions about the accommodation (see Figure 11). Your student will be an adult who can decide for themselves whether what you are offering is suitable for them and ask you direct for any further information. The arrangement is a private one between you and the student, with the college only passing on details.

If you are intending to provide host family accommodation then it is rather different. The organisation has a responsibility to select the right kind of host families who will look after their students. Therefore the questions are, of necessity, more detailed and personal as they need to know more about everyone in the house (see Figure 12). Your application will be followed up by a home visit.

HOST FAMILY APPLICATION FORM

Surname:_____First name:_____ Mr/Mrs/Miss/Ms

Address:_____

_____

Age:_____Religion:_____

Occupation:_____Hours of employment:_____

Husband/Wife/Partner's surname_____ First name:_____

Age:_____Religion_____

Occupation:_____Hours of employment:_____

Are there any other adults living in the house? Yes/No

If yes, please specify number and sex:_____ Relationship_____

Children living at home: Number boys_____ Ages_____
                         Number girls_____ Ages_____

Pets: Yes/No If yes give details:_____

Accommodation: Flat/terraced/house/semi-detached house/detached house

Number of student rooms: Singles_____ Twin_____

Dates when accommodation will *not* be available: from:____ to:____

Type of heating:_____   Do you have shower/bath/both?

Student preferences: Male/female   Smoker/non-smoker
                        Nationality:

Could you provide any special dietary requirements, eg vegetarian: Yes/No.

Any comments:

Fig. 12. Example of a host family application form.

HOME VETTING VISITS

Before entrusting their students to you many organisations will want to send someone to come and look at your room and see what sort of a person you are. This will be the case particularly for:

- host family accommodation for students from overseas
- any students under 16
- organisations requiring a specific standard of accommodation.

Arrangements will be made for a student accommodation or welfare officer to visit at a mutually convenient time. The purpose of his or her visit should be to:

- make sure the room offered is clean and comfortable
- see that the facilities are adequate
- check there are no dangerous hazards
- look for a friendly, warm and welcoming atmosphere
- explain fully what is expected of you and provide you with any guidelines
- give you details about payment
- advise you what to do if there is a problem
- answer any questions you may have.

It has to be said that these visits vary considerably from one organisation to another. Some are no more than flying visits with only a cursory glance at the room and certainly no time for questions to be asked. Others are more thorough; the accommodation officer will ask to see the bathroom, toilet and kitchen, want to know about who else is living in the house and make time to answer any queries. She or he may ask for further details about anything you have put on your application form.

What is expected of a host family?

As mentioned earlier, families hosting students from overseas are expected to provide more than just board and lodgings. They are expected to take the student into their home as one of the family, show an interest in them, spend time talking with them and generally have their welfare at heart. Having a kind and caring family, where the student is made to feel at home, makes all the difference to the student's stay in Britain. Indeed, it is a major factor in colouring their perception of Britain in general.

CODE OF PRACTICE FOR HOMESTAY
ACCOMMODATION PROVIDERS

1. To encourage the student to speak English as much as possible in my/our home.

2. To encourage the student to feel at home and to treat him/her as a member of the family rather than as a paying guest.

3. Not to host another student of the same native language at the same time unless by special arrangement with both the students and their schools/centres.

4. To provide a clean and comfortable student room meeting the physical requirements laid down by the British Council.

5. To provide a home environment in which it is possible for the student to carry on his/her English studies properly.

6. To provide the student with a balanced and appropriate diet.

7. To show due concern for the welfare, safety and security of the student during his/her stay.

8. To give the student reasonable and regular access to bathroom and laundry facilities.

9. To maintain a close liaison with the student's school/centre and so be in a position to help to resolve any problems that the student may encounter during his/her stay.

10. To respect the student's different cultural background and be sensitive to the particular needs of the student.

Fig. 13. Code of Practice for Homestay Accommodation Providers.

If you are hosting, in effect you are showing 'this is how we live in Britain'. You can be sure that every aspect of your student's stay will be reported back to family and friends in their own country. This means that you are helping to project a certain image of Britain abroad. Because this image is very important in attracting further students, it naturally follows that good host families are also very important.

The Homestay Code of Practice

Four organisations involved in promoting the teaching of English as a foreign language in Britain have produced a ten-point Code of Practice setting minimum standards expected of host families. These organisations are:

- The **British Council**
- **ARELS** (The Association of Recognised English Language Services)
- **BASELT** (The British Association of State English Language Teaching)
- The **British Tourist Authority**.

The British Council
The function of the British Council is to promote cultural, educational and technical cooperation between Britain and other countries. It will therefore help promote those language schools or colleges which have met its strict criteria and become accredited establishments. If your student's language school or college advertises as 'Recognised or validated by the British Council' you will know that it has passed regular stringent inspection procedures and meets high standards.

ARELS and BASELT
Once recognised, schools or colleges may become members of ARELS or BASELT which are the two leading professional associations in English language teaching, representing the private and state sectors respectively. If you provide host family accommodation for an ARELS or BASELT member establishment you will be asked to sign an agreement that you will abide by the ARELS/BASELT **Homestay Code of Practice** (see Figure 13).

CORRESPONDING WITH AN OVERSEAS STUDENT

With young language school students you are particularly asked to

- table for private study and adequate hanging and drawer space for clothes
- adequate heating and lighting
- adequate washing facilities and access to the bathroom as a member of the household, with bath/shower available daily
- change of bed linen each week and a good supply of blankets
- sufficiently spacious bedroom, adequately equipped and with natural light
- a proper state of cleanliness and repair in the home.

Fig. 14. British Council's student's room requirements.

write to them before they come to stay. All they will know about you so far is usually just your name, address and telephone number. Many parents are extremely worried about where their son or daughter will be staying and what the family will be like. A short welcoming letter will make them feel much happier and give the student a little more idea of what to expect. If you have teenagers of your own, it can be a good idea for them to write instead of you.

What can I write about?

It's not necessary, or advisable, to write a lot, and you should keep your sentences short and simple. Remember that, although some students are reasonably fluent in our language, others have a very limited grasp of it and may struggle to understand your letter. Here are a few suggestions of what you might include.

- Say you are looking forward to the visit.
- Tell them a little about your family.
- Let them know if you have any pets.
- Briefly describe your type of house.
- Mention anything interesting about your town.
- Tell them about any family hobbies.
- Suggest they write you a letter with a few details about themselves.

- Perhaps ask them if there is any food they particularly don't like or are unable to eat – although bear in mind that they may not know what English food is like.

Usually the student will happily write back, perhaps sending a photo. Writing a letter is good English practice and you will have started getting to know each other.

If you don't like writing letters, and many people don't, you could instead send a picture postcard of your town. Some organisations even provide their own postcards for you with a picture of a typical English family scene on it. Just write something simple on the back like 'I hope you will enjoy staying with us, we are looking forward to your visit very much. Please write and tell us about yourself.' If there is room you could include the names of all the family members with the ages of any children.

Whatever you write, you can be sure it will be eagerly received by your student and probably read, re-read and shown around to family and friends.

QUESTIONS AND ANSWERS

I have my details registered with the local college. Am I obliged to accept the first student who comes to look at my spare room?

No. You are under no obligation. After all it's your home and you have the right to turn down anyone you feel might not be suitable to live in it. You should remember also that, equally, the student has the right to turn down the accommodation if it's not what they want.

Can I still be accepted for host family accommodation if I go out to work?

This will depend on the hours you work, the age of the student and the policy of the school you've applied to. With adult students it's usually not a problem unless you work hours which would prevent you from providing a meal at a reasonable time. With junior students (under 16) they should not be expected to come home to an empty house and there should ideally always be an adult around.

CHECKLIST

- Start looking for accommodation wanted advertisements.

- If you are placing an advertisement make sure it is worded carefully.

- Carefully complete any application or registration forms and return them promptly.

- Expect a vetting visit if you are hosting.

- Make sure you have all the information you require about the student and from the organisation.

- Don't forget to write a letter of welcome if appropriate.

CASE STUDIES

Angela and Tony apply to a language school

Angela and Tony see a language school advertisement, for host families for teenage students, in their local paper. Angela telephones to request an application form and this arrives after a few days.

Once the form is sent back they have to wait until the accommodation officer comes to visit. This is about two weeks later. She has a look at the lounge, kitchen and bathroom as well as the bedroom, and has a good chat to Angela about what is expected of host families. Everything goes well and the accommodation officer says she would be pleased to place students here for the summer. She says she will probably be able to give them at least two pairs for three to four weeks each and the details will be sent in due course.

Angela and Tony had already decided that they were happy to take boys or girls and did not mind what nationality. After about a month they receive a contract offering them two 14-year-old boys, Marcus and Sebastian, for three weeks starting in June. Angela writes a short letter of welcome to each of them.

Claire places her own advert

Claire types out an advertisement on a postcard and asks at her local hospital if it could be put on the staff noticeboard. It is accepted and, although she expects a small charge, is told there is nothing to pay.

Two days later she receives a phone call from Lucy Wilson, who is a 20-year-old student nurse. Lucy is at the moment living in the nurses' home but doesn't like it and wants to move out. A time is arranged for Lucy to call and look at the flat the next day. Lucy is disappointed that the room is not bigger but says she would like to take it. Claire feels Lucy will not be any bother and so, after a short discussion, agrees she can move in as soon as she likes.

Claire is lucky in that she has found someone easily and without any expense or delay.

Helen registers with the university

Helen contacts the university accommodation office and is given a registration form to complete with full details of what she is offering. Helen describes her accommodation as 'bed and breakfast with evening meals by arrangement'. She knows enough about student life to realise students don't want to be tied down to fixed meal-times but that there may be occasions when a meal would be appreciated.

Helen's details are passed on and she receives a telephone call from Amanda Hartley, aged 18, who will be starting as an undergraduate in October. Amanda has missed the chance of accommodation in the university halls of residence because of applying too late. She is interested in Helen's room and is happy to take it without viewing.

Barbara phones up on spec

Barbara has never seen an advertisement from the nearby teaching training college for accommodation, but telephones on spec to enquire. They tell her that they may be able to use her if she lives near, which she does. Barbara is then asked for her details over the phone and specifies she is looking for a non-smoking lady who is a dog-lover.

She accepts a booking from Lisa Duncan, who is in her late twenties and assures her she doesn't smoke and loves dogs! The arrangement is for one term only to start with and matters are confirmed in writing.

DISCUSSION POINTS

1.   If there is more than one local establishment requiring student accommodation which would be the best choice for you, and why?

2.   What questions would you need to ask before agreeing to take in a student?

3.   How do you feel about someone you haven't met moving in?

4
Sorting out Practical Matters

When making your arrangements there are certain official and practical matters to be gone into and it is important that none of these are overlooked.

SIGNING CONTRACTS AND AGREEMENTS

Things you need to know and agree

1. What period the accommodation is for.

2. How much money you are going to be paid.

3. When it will be paid.

4. What meals and services you are undertaking to provide.

5. What period of notice is required if either party wants to terminate the arrangement.

6. Any specific arrangements.

It is not essential to have a written agreement. Many people are happy with just a verbal one. However, it can be useful to have something in writing so that there are no misunderstandings and this is up to you.

Organisations which are paying you will have their own contracts or booking confirmations (see Figure 15). Other organisations, such as universities, will often advise you on agreements or even have agreement forms for you to purchase and fill out yourself. You can also draw up your own simple agreement (see Figure 16).

• The important thing is that arrangements are clearly understood between you and the organisation or student.

HOST FAMILY ACCOMMODATION – BOOKING FORM

We are pleased to offer the following booking:

Host family name and address:

Student details:

Name: Age: Male/Female

Address:

Nationality:

Accommodation requirements

Date from: Date to:
(Arrival time to be advised later)

Type of accommodation: Single room/shared room

Full board (3 meals per day to include packed lunches on week-days).

Access to laundry facilities

Payment rate: per night

Special requirements:

*eg   Non-smoking house
        No pets*

Signed: .... Date: ....
for Language School

I accept this booking on the above terms.

Signed: .... Date: ....

Please sign and return one copy of this form to us as soon as possible. Thank you.

Fig. 15. Example of a host family booking form.

AGREEMENT

between... (householder)

and... (student)

dated:...

in respect of part-board accommodation at:

....

consisting of: Bed and Breakfast
Tea and coffee as required
Single room with washbasin

Fee payable: £___ per calendar month

payable___ monthly in advance

commencing___

to also include: heating
lighting
electricity
use of bathroom, laundry and kitchen facilities

A holiday reduction of £___ will apply for any period of 7 consecutive nights away

Arrangements:

room will be cleaned and bed-linen changed weekly
extra meals by request at additional agreed charge
permission must be asked before visitors are invited
no smoking is allowed in the house
no loud music which might create disturbance
cost of telephone calls to be reimbursed at time of call
any breakages to be reported and paid for
four weeks' notice of request to vacate or intention to leave
(except in cases of non-payment or unacceptable
behaviour when reduced or no notice will be given)

Signed:.. (householder)

Signed:.. (student)

Fig. 16. Example of a private agreement.

58

- All agreements or contracts should be in duplicate: one for you and one for whoever is making the payments.

- Both of you should check that you understand everything and are happy with the agreement.

- Both of you should sign and date the agreement.

AGREEING FEES AND PAYMENTS

Although you will not make a fortune from students you can make a steady and useful profit that can make all the difference to your income. It can help you afford that dream holiday or new car. It can enable you to meet your bills on time without struggling.

How much can I expect to be paid or to charge?

Your fees or charges will vary according to
(a)   the area you live in
(b)   what you are offering
(c)   the organisation concerned.

- Two organisations in the same area can offer different amounts for the same facilities, so you need to shop around as you would with anything else.

- For example, language school payments usually average £6.50 to £10 per night. You may get a lower payment from one school for providing full board than you would with another where you only need to provide half board.

- The lowest payments are usually for shared rooms and long-term placements, but, on the other hand, you will often get full payment for any weeks a long-term student is away on holiday, such as at Christmas or Easter, to boost your profits.

- If you are offering a room or lodgings through a college or university accommodation office, you will usually be given guidelines on expected charges. Again, these vary.

- Remember, proximity to campus is a factor in deciding the fee.

- As a rough guide, rents average £35–£40 for a room including heating and use of cooking and bathroom facilities, and around £45–£70 for part or full board.

- If you are arranging things completely privately you can of course charge whatever you think fit. However, it needs to be in line with similar accommodation in the area or you may find you have no takers. Remember most students are trying to balance a low budget and accommodation costs are a major concern.

Arranging the frequency of payment

Most organisations will not make any payment in advance.

- If you are, for example, having summer students for a three-week stay you may get the whole amount for the stay after about ten days.

- Alternatively, at the end of the first week you may be paid for two weeks with the final week kept until the end.

- For long-stay students payments are usually made on a fixed monthly basis, for example the last Friday in the month, and start about two weeks after the student arrives.

- Different organisations do vary in their payment methods and it is important that you know what they are.

If a student is paying you direct then you need to arrange the frequency between you. It is usual to ask for these payments in advance and to decide on either weekly or monthly. These arrangements are a personal matter between you and your student.

Giving receipts

Although a student paying by cheque will have the cheque counterfoil as proof of payment, it's a good idea to give a receipt and keep a copy for your own records. You can buy proper receipt books or just use a small duplicate book. Make sure you always specify the period covered by the payment.

RECEIVED with thanks from: *Amanda Hartley*

The sum of: *£185*

Board and lodging charge for the period 1st to 31st October 199X

Signed: *Helen Darrell*   Date: *1st October 199X*

Fig. 17. Example of a receipt.

LOOKING AT TAX AND INSURANCE

These are things which may make us all groan but should never be ignored. Spending a little time now to make sure your affairs are in order can save you a lot of worry and headaches later on.

Do I have to pay income tax?

It's wise to check into your income tax liability with your local tax office. You may well find you are exempt, in which case your mind is set at rest. If you find you are not, then remember it is an offence not to declare taxable income.

Many people think they can easily avoid paying tax on income earned from having students. However, be warned that the Inland Revenue can, and sometimes does, ask any organisation for details of payments made to individuals. Organisations then have a legal obligation to divulge these details. It makes sense to find out exactly where you stand.

The Rent a Room scheme

The **Rent a Room scheme** has been introduced to help people letting out a room in their own home.

- Under the scheme you are allowed to receive a total of £3,250 (1996 figure) gross income in each tax year, completely tax-free, from letting out furnished rooms, or having lodgers, in your own home.

- This figure is quite separate from any other income you may have.

- Please note this figure applies to *income*, not profit.

- Unless your total is more than this, you have no income tax liability to worry about.

- This figure applies whether you are just letting a room, or providing full board and a laundry service. You cannot claim further allowances for extra expenses under the scheme.

If, however, you take two or more students for most of the year you may find that the combined income exceeds this figure and that you have income tax liability. You then have the choice of whether to come under the Rent a Room scheme, or of being taxed in the normal way on your profit after any expenses and allowances. Which method is to your advantage will depend on the amount of profit you are making. Your local tax office will be able to give you further advice on this.

Remember, even if your income from taking in students exceeds this figure, you still may not necessarily have to pay tax. This will depend on other income and what allowances you have, which can vary from person to person. If you have any doubts, check with your tax office.

Maintaining adequate insurance

● Are you insured?

● Do you know exactly what you're covered for?

● Have you reviewed your policies lately to see if they still cover your present needs?

● Have you thought that you might need extra cover because of a student living in your house?

● If so, have you done anything about it?

If you are able to honestly answer yes to all these questions then you're totally on the ball and well organised. But you would also be in the minority.

The vast majority of people don't have adequate cover. Some, and a surprisingly high percentage, don't have any insurance at all. They happily take the chance that nothing will happen and then, when it does, it's too late. They might save a few pounds by not paying the premiums but could end up facing a bill for thousands. Is it really worth the risk?

Imagine the following scenarios.

● Your student has an accident in your home and is seriously injured. If it can be proved you have been negligent then you could be sued for thousands of pounds. What would you do if you don't have insurance to cover it?

● Your student accidentally sets fire to the house. Are you covered for this?

● Your student has caused deliberate damage. You may think you can make the student pay, but can you? Perhaps it can't be proved or they've left the country. Will your insurance company pay out?

• Your water tank suddenly bursts and repair is a big expense. You have to get it fixed quickly or your student could well decide to move out. If someone is paying to live in your home they don't have to put up with unreasonable inconvenience.

Insurance policies vary so you need to contact your insurer to find out exactly what you would be covered for with a student living in your home. You may already be covered on some points, but need to pay a small additional premium for others. Don't leave it – check it out right away. A quick phone call is all it takes.

Theft
Usually you will only be covered for theft if there has been a break-in. This means that you are not likely to be covered if your student steals from you. Make sure you don't put temptation in the way by leaving money or valuables around.

Your student's possessions
Your household contents insurance is unlikely to cover your student's possessions. Therefore it is up to them to make their own arrangements for these.

ENSURING SAFETY AND SECURITY

It is your responsibility to make your home as safe and secure as possible for everyone living there. The more people living in a house, the more chance there is of an accident being caused.

Carrying out safety checks
Too many needless injuries and deaths are caused in the home each year simply because basic safety precautions are not taken. Don't let your household add to these statistics.

Gas appliances
1.   You have a legal responsibility to ensure gas safety.

2.   All gas appliances should be serviced and safety-checked each year by a qualified gas fitter.

3. Some organisations won't take you on their approved list unless you can show a safety certificate.

4. Check for danger signals yourself such as black marks around fires.

5. Consider buying a carbon monoxide detector.

6. Leave repairs to the professionals.

Electrical equipment

1. Regularly inspect all your electrical appliances, such as heaters, irons and hair-dryers.

2. Look for frayed flexes or loose plugs.

3. Check for scorch marks around sockets, or plugs over-heating.

4. Think about using a power-breaker to safeguard you in case of faulty equipment.

5. Don't overload your electricity sockets by using too many items.

6. Never plug an electrical appliance into a light fitting.

7. Make sure you know how to fit a plug.

8. Check that the correct fuse for the appliance is fitted: the rule is 3 amp for appliances up to 720 watts and 13 amp over 720 watts.

9. When was your wiring last checked? Electricity boards often do this free.

10. Make sure any electrical work is carried out by a qualified electrician.

11. Don't put cables under carpets where they can be walked on.

12. Don't put heaters where they can be knocked over, and keep them well away from furniture and furnishings.

13. Switch off appliances when not in use and remove plugs.

14. Look for the BEAB approved label on new equipment. This means that it has been tested and approved by the British Electrotechnical Approvals Board.

General safety
1. Look around the home for potential safety hazards.

2. Get anything dangerous repaired immediately.

3. Check stairs for loose carpeting.

4. Make sure you have a fire extinguisher and that you know how it works.

5. Make sure everyone knows what to do in case of fire.

6. Make sure there is a window which can be easily opened in each room in case you need to get out of it.

7. Think about having more than one telephone extension so that you can call for help more quickly in an emergency.

Being careful in the kitchen
1. A high percentage of accidents happen in the kitchen. No matter now careful you are very few households can claim never to have had some sort of accident.

2. Make sure your student knows how to use the cooker. Remember some students may not be used to cooking and many overseas students will never have even seen a gas cooker before.

3. Impress on your student never to leave a chip pan unattended; this is one of the major causes of home fires.

Smoke detectors
In a house fire, smoke is the biggest killer. It burns up oxygen and generates lethal gases. If you are asleep don't think the smell of smoke will wake you up: smoke contains carbon monoxide which will put you into a deeper sleep. Smoke detectors cost only a few pounds and could save your lives.

• *Every* home should have smoke detectors, normally at least one on each floor.

- The recommended places to fit them are: in the hallway between the living and sleeping area in a flat or bungalow, at the bottom of the staircase and on the upstairs landing for a house. Additional alarms could also be fitted in bedrooms or the lounge.

- If your home doesn't have smoke detectors, you are strongly advised to get at least one or two right away.

- If money is short get just one now and another in a couple of weeks.

- Whatever you do, *don't let your home go without one.*

- Remember also that smoke detectors need testing regularly to make sure they are in full working order: do this once a week.

Knowledge of emergency procedures

If you have overseas students remember that they are likely to be unfamiliar with our emergency services.

- Make sure they know how, and when, to dial 999. It is always better to be safe than sorry.

- Make sure everyone knows what to do in the event of a fire.

- If you need any advice about fire safety contact your local fire brigade, who will be pleased to help. They will also let you have some free leaflets and you can put one in your student's room.

First aid

Make sure you have a first aid kit and some basic first aid knowledge. You can buy a ready-made first aid kit or alternatively make up your own, buying a couple of items here and there to spread the cost. Knowledge of basic first aid is something that everyone should have. 'If only I had known what to do!' is often the cry after an accident or when someone becomes unwell.

Give yourself a little test. Would you know what to do if someone:

(a)   Has collapsed and is unconscious?
(b)   Has stopped breathing?
(c)   Is cut and bleeding heavily?
(d)   Has fallen and is in acute pain?
(e)   Has been burned?
(f)   Has swallowed something dangerous?

If the answer is No then it's worth thinking about attending a first aid course. Both the British Red Cross and St John run these regularly. As well as full courses running for about twelve sessions, there are often one-day courses to teach you the basics.

Personal safety

Warn your student about the dangers of coming home late at night alone. Advise them to keep to well-lit streets or to take a taxi. Younger students are particularly vulnerable both to theft and assault, and you should ensure with the under-16s that you know where they are going and that they are home by 10.30–11 pm.

Making your home more secure

Don't invite burglars by making it easy for them. Reduce the risks of a break-in by taking a few sensible precautions.

Checking doors

Make sure your doors are strong and sturdy and that any glass panels are laminated glass which is difficult to break.

Check your locks; install a mortice deadlock for maximum security. A deadlock can only be opened with a key so, if a burglar gets in through a window, he cannot open the door to walk out with your television set.

Installing window locks

Many new windows now come with key-operated security locks as standard. If not, you can get inexpensive window locks from DIY shops. Easily visible locks may deter burglars because they prefer not to break the glass and risk someone hearing. Don't have locks fitted and then go out and leave the window open!

Taking care of keys

All adult students will need a key to your house. So will junior ones unless you can guarantee there is always someone around to let them in. Impress upon your student the need to take care of your key and to tell you immediately if it should be lost.

Some families have thought they were being helpful by putting their name and address on the key tag. This is a big mistake and should be avoided at all costs: if the key is lost, and falls into the wrong hands, there is an open invitation to a burglar or worse.

If your front door has the sort of secure lock which can only be opened from the inside by a key, make sure that a spare one is kept nearby but out of sight and that everyone knows where this is. If there is a fire, precious moments can be wasted while people hunt for keys so that they can get out.

KEEPING RECORDS

It's often useful to keep records of:

(a)   your student's details
(b)   payments received
(c)   household expenditure
(d)   an inventory of items in your student's room.

There is no need for them to be complicated, just simple and straightforward.

Student details
It might be useful if you keep to hand:

* the student's home address and telephone number
* date of birth
* name of who to contact in the event of an emergency.

You never know when you might need these details: perhaps your student could be involved in an accident, taken ill or go missing. You could use a small, inexpensive notebook. Pieces of paper tend to get lost and you don't need to go to the expense of index cards. It's also useful if you know about any chronic medical condition they may have or any regular prescribed medication they are on.

Record of payments received
A simple cash book is useful for you to keep track of your payments, particularly if you don't have copies of receipts because you are paid direct. This acts as a check in the case of any query and so that you know payments are up-to-date. Mistakes can happen and cheques can go astray in the post. It's easy to forget exact dates when payments were received. A record of payments may also be needed for tax purposes.

Household expenditure records
Some people like to keep careful track of all their expenditure and this is particularly important if you are claiming any sort of

23/6/9X	Payment for period 20/6/9X - 3/7/9X	112	00
13/7/9X	Payment for period 4/7/0X - 10/7/9X	56	00

Fig. 18. Example of payment record.

expenses. It's also useful to help work out your profit margins. Good stationers have household expenditure record books. These are divided into different sections for you to complete with details of amounts paid for gas, electricity, telephone, decorating, food bills and so on. You can then see at a glance just how much extra you are spending with an additional person in the house.

Keeping inventories
Many people don't bother with this, but it can be useful to include an inventory with any agreement. Then you can check at the end of any stay whether all the items are still there and in good condition.

QUESTIONS AND ANSWERS

What happens if I sign an agreement to have a student for an academic year but then half-way through I am unable to continue for some reason?

Such agreements are not legally binding and it would simply be terminated. Sometimes it is unavoidable if there is a problem such as illness or a major family trauma. Obviously it is helpful if you can give reasonable notice, but organisations realise that this is sometimes not possible and they should have emergency accommodation arrangements for their students.

Should I provide a separate lock and key to my student's room?

No. If the student is living as one of the family they certainly will not expect it since it is not usual for normal family rooms to have locks.

If they are not living as one of the family then you may decide to provide a lock and key, and many students will prefer a room which they can lock. However, this is entirely up to you. There is no obligation but, if you do, make sure you have a spare key at all times for yourself.

I am on income support. How will this be affected if I have a student?

You must inform the office which pays your benefit. You are allowed a certain amount towards the cost of your student's food and other expenses before your income support is reduced. Check this before you start.

CHECKLIST

● Make sure you know what your payments will be and when they will be made to you.

● Be quite sure about what you have agreed with your student on what is to be provided by you.

● Check your income tax liability.

● Make sure you have adequate insurance.

● Do a room-by-room safety check.

● Make sure that all windows and doors are secure.

● Keep a record of all important transactions connected with taking in a student.

CASE STUDIES

Angela and Tony are safety conscious

As responsible parents Angela and Tony have done all they can to make their home safe. With two young children who are into everything they have to take special precautions. Their gas fires are serviced and safety-checked each year and have guards around them. They have no portable heaters which can be knocked over, unused electric sockets have socket covers and there are safety gates for the stairs.

When Marcus and Sebastian arrive Angela or Tony will talk to them about what to do if there should be a fire, and also warn them when they go out to remember that cars travel on the left-hand side of the road here.

Claire wants advance payment

When Claire and Lucy make the arrangements for Lucy to move in they have a verbal agreement only. Claire tells Lucy clearly that she wants paying monthly in advance, on the same date each month, starting from the day she moves in. She wants Lucy to give her four weeks' notice if she decides to move out and says she will give Lucy the same if she wants her to leave. This is a mutual agreement between the two of them and, if they both keep to it, means that Claire would have time to find a replacement and Lucy would have time to find somewhere else when necessary.

Lucy pays Claire the money by cheque. Claire says that a receipt is not necessary because Lucy will have her cheque counterfoil and bank statement as proof of payment. Lucy is quite happy about this.

Helen buys some smoke alarms

Helen has often thought that she really should get some smoke alarms but, like many people, has just not done so. It's one of those things which it is easy to keep putting off. Now that she is having a student, and has been thinking more about safety and security aspects, she decides to get two smoke alarms: one for the downstairs hall and one for the upstairs landing. Helen buys these next time she is shopping in town from a DIY store. She checks they conform to the British Standard. The instructions remind her to test the alarms each week.

Barbara's burglar deterrents

Living on her own and in a bungalow has made Barbara more security-minded. All her windows are vulnerable and therefore she has key-operated locks on each one. Her doors have mortice deadlocks, bolts and security chains. Barbara does also have one more very useful burglar deterrent – her dog!

DISCUSSION POINTS

1. What would be a realistic figure for you to spend on insurance premiums?

2. What steps could you take to make your home safer and more secure?

3. What sort of records might you consider keeping?

5
Settling In

Finally, the day has come when your student is due to arrive. If you haven't met, then of course you will be wondering just what this person will be like. You may well begin to worry.

- Will you get on together?

- Will he or she fit in?

- Are there going to be any problems?

- Suppose it doesn't work out?

It's natural to feel a little apprehensive about these things. However, *think positive*. Remember also your student will probably be feeling exactly the same and wondering about *you*.

MAKING YOUR STUDENT WELCOME

It's your home and therefore it is up to you to make your student feel welcome and at ease. Perhaps it is his or her first time of living away from home or of being in this country. Everything is going to be different for them and you need to help make the first few days as smooth as possible.

Preparing for arrival

Hopefully an arrival time has been arranged and you have been notified of this. Very often, though, there are travel delays so don't be surprised if your student is later than expected. Be warned that arrivals from overseas can sometimes be late at night or even in the early hours of the morning – which is not the best time to meet someone!

Collecting your student
If you are having younger language school students you usually find that you are expected to meet them off the coach. Whilst you wait for it to arrive at the designated place is a good time to get talking to other host families.

Experienced ones will happily recount stories of their previous students and speculate about the new ones. By the time the coach eventually turns up you have often gained some invaluable tips!

The teenagers will pour off the coach in an excited, chattering stream, eyeing up the families and trying to guess which one is theirs. If you've already exchanged photos of course it helps. Mounds of luggage will come out of the coach, then one of the language school representatives will call out the names and match people up. After that it's smiles and introductions and into the car home.

Home delivery
Some organisations will bring the student to your door in their own mini-bus, or organise a taxi. This arrangement is usual for adult students and of course saves you the inconvenience of having to go out to meet them.

Travelling independently
Many students will make their way to you independently or, perhaps, be brought by their families. Some host families kindly offer to meet those who travel by public transport and this is always appreciated.

First impressions
You take an immediate liking to some people. You may not be so sure about others. However, don't make your judgement too quickly and don't go by the way they are dressed. Wearing outrageous clothes doesn't mean your student will behave outrageously!

You both need time to get to know and adjust to each other. Remember also the student may be:

• tired after a long journey
• shy
• if from overseas, nervous of speaking English.

Breaking the ice
Although a great many students will be exuberant and chatty, some will not and need more drawing out. If you have children they are a

USEFUL INFORMATION

Welcome to our home!
We hope you will enjoy staying here and that you will be comfortable. To help you, here is some information you might find useful.

Mealtimes
Breakfast is from 7.30 to 8.30 am. If you want it later than this you may help yourself but please clear away and wash up afterwards.
Dinner is usually at 6.30 pm.
Please let us know if you are going to be late because of an outing.

Drinks
You can help yourselves to tea, coffee or orange squash when you want.

Laundry
Please ask when you want to use the washing machine.

Bathroom
Please do not have a bath between 7 and 7.30 in the morning. Thank you.

Coming in at night
If you are under 16 please be home by 10.30 Monday to Friday or by 11 pm at weekends.

Telephone
Please ask first if you need to use the telephone.

Problems
Please let us know if you have any problems and we will try to help.

Please note that smoking is not allowed in your room.

Enjoy your stay!

Fig. 19. Information for students.

great help at breaking the ice. Someone coming to stay is usually a source of great excitement and interest. They have a healthy curiosity to know everything. Most will not be afraid to ask questions (and may need some restraining in this respect!) and are refreshingly frank.

A few dos and don'ts

- Do offer the use of your telephone to call home soon after arrival. Many families are anxiously waiting to hear of their offspring's safe arrival.

- Don't worry if you have a student who seems only able to say 'yes' or 'no'. This state of affairs rarely lasts for long once they get to know you!

- Do give them a little time to settle down.

- Don't expect them to immediately understand and remember everything you tell them.

EXPLAINING HOUSE RULES

Although you may not feel the need for a lot of rules and regulations, there are some points you should make clear from the start to avoid misunderstandings and potential problems. Remember, *you* are the one who makes the rules and these should be explained politely and firmly within the first day or two.

To make sure points are not forgotten, it's a good idea to do a short notice and pin it in the student's room (see Figure 19).

The following are the main points you need to cover.

Sharing the house

Make clear which rooms the student can feel free to use beside their own. Are they welcome to use your lounge whenever they want? Are there rooms you don't want them to go into? What about the garden?

Respecting meal times

Your student needs to know what time to be in for meals where these are provided and should turn up promptly. A common complaint is that students are never in for their meals on time. The reason for this is that they are usually too busy having a good time and don't realise how late it is. Often, too, we eat earlier here than some overseas students are used to. Although you are expected to allow a little flexibility for outings and special occasions, ask him or her to let you know well in advance:

(a)   if they will be out or late for a meal
(b)   when a packed lunch is required
(c)   if they need an early meal.

Not to tell you is simply bad manners and can lead to understandable frustration and annoyance on your part.

Taking snacks
Be quite clear about whether students are allowed to help themselves to drinks and sandwiches, or whether they must ask first. Be quite specific about *exactly* what they are allowed to have without asking. 'Help yourself to a drink' could mean all your milk destined for breakfast the next day vanishing, or even your drinks cabinet being depleted!

Coming in at night
Adult students will expect freedom to come home whatever time they like, or to stay out if they wish to. However, you should explain that if they come in late you expect that they will be quiet, not bang doors or make any noise which will wake the household. Do not hesitate to tell them if you are disturbed. Also it is courteous to tell you if they are not coming home overnight.

In the case of younger language school students, the schools usually specify a time for them to be home according to their age. Be warned that the vast majority totally ignore this! However, most host mothers feel a responsibility for their students and will not like to go to bed until they are safely in. This can mean sitting up until the early hours when you are longing to go to sleep. You therefore need to speak firmly about this and warn them that you will contact the school if they persist in being late. This will usually do the trick; otherwise ask your student leader to have a word.

Using the telephone
Be sure to explain the arrangements for using the telephone. Your student should always ask permission to use it and pay you for the call. You can either estimate the cost and charge accordingly, or ask the operator in advance for the **charge advice** service. If you have an overseas student wanting to call home they should make a **reverse**

charge (collect) call. Some come with a special number to use which automatically reverses the charge.

It's advisable to have an itemised telephone bill so that you can see what calls have been made and check them. With a long-stay student you may agree that they pay you when the bill comes in. Remember to add VAT as this is charged separately on telephone bills.

Don't forget that even incoming calls can be a problem. Teenagers like to talk and can be quite oblivious to the fact that someone else might want to use the phone. Usually you will be the one to answer the phone and it's quite easy to say 'Don't be too long – I'm expecting a call' or something like that as you hand it over.

Allowing friends to visit

It is up to you to decide whether to allow friends to visit and at what times. You may stipulate that this is only when agreed by prior arrangement and when you are home. You may also consider a ruling such as no visitors after 10pm, or whatever time you think reasonable. It's wise to lay down some sort of ground rules, otherwise you could find the visitors are still there in the morning.

Smoking

If you are a smoker yourself you will probably be quite happy to accommodate a smoker. Or you may not be a smoker yourself but decide to allow smoking, perhaps in designated rooms only.

However, many people find smoking extremely unpleasant and do not wish to have smokers in their home. If this is the case you should already have made it clear before accepting your student. It does sometimes happen that you are sent a smoker in spite of a specific request to the contrary, or perhaps a student decides to start smoking. You have every right to insist they do not do so inside the house.

Room-cleaning and bed-making

Be clear about what the arrangements are. Generally this is that:

- The room is cleaned and the bed linen changed on a weekly basis.
- The students are expected to make their own beds on a daily basis.

The exception to this is if you have a special 'executive level' student who might be paying a considerably higher fee, and so would be entitled to a daily cleaning and bed-making service. With long-term students you may consider they can easily clean their own rooms. Points in favour of this are:

(a) It saves you having to do it.
(b) If other members of the family look after their own rooms, why can't the student?

Points in favour of doing it yourself are:

(a) You are sure it is done.
(b) It gives you a chance to keep an eye on the room and make sure there is no damage.

SHARING THE BATHROOM

Use of the bathroom needs to be organised if you are to live in harmony. Otherwise it can end up a battle zone! The more people in the house, the longer the queue will be. In the mornings, with everyone rushing off to work, college or school it could well mean *someone* is going to be late.

Although you should allow for a daily bath or shower, it is quite reasonable to either agree a regular time for this or expect your student to ask first if it's convenient, so explain right at the beginning if there are any restrictions. You do not want one person using all the hot water or leisurely soaking for hours while other people are kept waiting. If you do not have a spare toilet then your problem will be compounded.

Understanding the arrangements

Although you may think things have been clearly explained, overseas students may misunderstand you completely. For example one lady, Judith, always asks her students to please not use the shower before 7 am or after 10 pm. This is quite a reasonable request. However, one student was using the shower as early as 5 am and waking everyone up. When Judith had a quiet word, it transpired that the student had got things the wrong way round. She thought she was not allowed to shower *between* 7 am and 10 pm and had been getting up early in order to comply with this request!

Allocating towels

It's surprising how many people will simply grab the nearest available towel after having a wash or bath, regardless of who it may belong to. Allocate towels to your students which can be kept in their own room and taken with them to the bathroom when required. Additionally, provide a small guest-towel in the bathroom for hands.

Cleaning the bath
Explain to your student that everyone is expected to clean out the bath after using it. It's important to show them what you use to do this with as otherwise you may find they inadvertently use your face flannel or the cloth you use to clean the toilet, not to mention shampoo or bath foam. With younger ones you may also need to show them how to do it. Remember some students will only be used to showers and quite likely will never have cleaned a bath out in their lives before. It's easiest to explain this when you are showing them the bathroom in the beginning.

LAUNDRY ARRANGEMENTS

'My electricity bills have rocketed since my student moved in.'
    'She uses the tumble dryer practically every day!'
    These are cries echoed by many host families and landladies. But usually it is because nothing has been clearly specified to the student about how often they can use the laundry facilities or the most effective way of use. Don't forget that some students may never have done their own laundry before.

Keeping the bills down
You may just assume that once or twice a week will be enough for anyone to use the washing machine. However, you could easily find your student wants to use it on almost a daily basis. This is not realistic and, particularly if they are using the tumble dryer, will certainly erode your profit margin quicker than anything else. Probably the cost will not even enter your student's head. After all, unless you are paying for something you don't usually worry about how expensive it is.

Charging extra
It is generally accepted that, because of the high cost of electricity and washing powder, you are entitled to charge extra for laundry if an allowance is not included in your payment. This can be either a weekly amount or a small fee each time your facilities are used. If you are actually providing a service by doing the washing and ironing yourself, you need to make an appropriately higher charge

to recompense for your time, or allow for it in your overall fee.

Providing radiator airers

It's certainly worth obtaining some of the type of small airers that hook over a radiator. These are inexpensive (under £5) but can save you money by enabling the smaller articles to be dried indoors at no extra cost.

Explaining things clearly

You need to make quite sure your student understands:

- That the washing machine must not be used for just a couple of items, only for full loads.

- How much washing powder to use and where to put it.

- That the tumble dryer, if used, should not be put on for longer than necessary.

- That if the weather is fine, and you have a washing line, the clothes should be dried outside.

- What days the laundry can be done.

These points are important to make the most economic use of your facilities. They will also help avoid potential wastages such as a student putting on your tumble dryer for two hours with just a few thin items in it and then happily going out whilst your electricity is wasting. Specifying set days to do laundry, particularly if there are a lot of people in the house, saves the machine being in use when *you* want to use it.

There are of course students who have their own ideas about laundry. Lynda came home from the shops to find all the windows of her house gaily festooned with drying underwear!

Some families, although a minority, do not allow use of their laundry facilities at all and expect their students to use the laundrette. This of course is up to you unless it is specified in your contract, which it sometimes is.

IDENTIFYING LOCAL AMENITIES

Besides telling them the best way to get to their place of study, your student will appreciate being shown or told the whereabouts of some or all of the following:

- post office and letter box
- public telephone, if they are not allowed to use yours or want to use phone-cards
- bank
- cashpoint
- bureau de change
- chemist
- shops
- cinema
- railway station
- bus stop and bus station
- sports centre
- place of worship
- tourist information centre
- the pub is usually one place they do not need any help to find!

Language schools usually give their students maps and arrange orientation sessions for them locally. You are generally expected to show the younger ones to school on their first day.

You will find that students find their way around quickly and easily. Before long they will know the area as well as – or sometimes even better than – you do!

QUESTIONS AND ANSWERS

I have heard that arrival dates sometimes get changed at the last minute. Is this so?

Yes, there are occasions when this is unavoidable. Hopefully, though, you would get advance warning. In the case of later arrivals you are still entitled to receive payment from the date originally agreed. If an earlier arrival is asked for then this will only be with your agreement and appropriate payment adjustment.

I'm worried about my student. She seems homesick and hasn't really settled down with us. What can I do?

Don't worry too much. Just try to be warm and friendly without fussing unduly. Spending time talking often helps. Once she has started the course and made new friends she will probably seem like a different person and start enjoying herself. It just takes longer with some than others.

At the end of the day, it's up to the student to be positive about this new experience and get the most out of it.

If you have a very young student and have cause to be really concerned then there is always a student leader to contact.

My student has really made herself at home. The trouble is that when she has a bath she helps herself liberally to my best toiletries. What's the best way of dealing with this?

There are just two choices. Remove them or confront her. However, you certainly should not have to move your own toiletries from your own bathroom! So the answer is to confront her immediately and ask her to stop. The longer you leave anything like this the more difficult it becomes to resolve. There's no need to make a big issue of it. Just get straight to the point and say something like, 'By the way, I notice you've been using my best bath foam. That's not for anyone else to use but me', or 'Would you mind buying your own bath foam and not using mine?' This approach is far better than shouting 'How dare you use my bath foam!'

CHECKLIST

• Make sure you have been notified of the arrival date and time.

• Let your student know about meal times, using the bathroom and other domestic arrangements.

• Explain clearly about what you allow and do not allow.

• Make sure your student understands about laundry arrangements.

• Help your student to find his/her way around.

CASE STUDIES

Marcus and Sebastian arrive

The boys are scheduled to arrive in the middle of the afternoon. Angela drives Tony to work in the morning so that she has the car to use to pick them up. She has to take both the children with her.

The coach is about half-an-hour late but then everything is sorted out quickly. Marcus and Sebastian are full of smiles as they shake hands. They are excited and enthusiastic about their stay. The luggage is crammed into the car with some difficulty and after several attempts. The boys are not shy, they make the children laugh and they are polite to Angela.

Once home they have a drink and unpack. Then the boys are eager to go out and explore right away. Angela suggests they telephone home first in case their mothers are worried. She tells them what time to be home for dinner and checks they have a map.

First impressions are that they are pleasant boys who look as if they will liven things up for the next three weeks!

Lucy moves in

A friend of Lucy's gives her a lift to Claire's with her luggage. Claire gives her a key and shows her one shelf in the fridge and one in the food cupboard which are allocated to her. She tells Lucy to make herself at home and breezes out shortly afterwards.

Lucy immediately finds there are not enough coat hangers in the wardrobe and puts these on her lists of things she needs. The friend suggests that hooks on the back of the door would help provide more hanging space. There's no heater but Lucy feels that Claire should provide this and resolves to ask her later.

The room is very small, but it's going to be home to Lucy and she makes the best of it. Once she has her posters on the walls it looks a lot better. With her bed made up and her radio cassette, tapes and bits and pieces arranged on top of the chest of drawers, it looks homely and cosy.

Amanda's parents come too

Amanda's parents bring her in the car as she has a good deal of luggage, including a computer and music system. They also want to see her safely settled in.

Helen makes them all welcome and offers tea. While Debbie helps Amanda with her luggage, Amanda's over-protective mother asks Helen to let her know immediately if there are any problems or concerns. She confides that she is worried about her daughter, an only child, being away from home for the first time but happy that Helen will be able to keep an eye on her.

Amanda herself seems quiet and shy, but is very much looking forward to university life and the freedom of being away from home.

Lisa feels at home

Lisa arrives independently in her own car. Barbara has been looking forward to her arrival and has a hot meal waiting. Lisa is grateful for this and they have a long chat whilst they are eating. They find each other easy to talk to. Lisa tells Barbara about her family and how much she wants to be a teacher. In turn Barbara tells Lisa about the job she had and how she now enjoys her reading and gardening.

Lisa is very pleased with her room and finds plenty of space for all her belongings. Barbara puts her suitcases in the loft so that they are out of the way. She thinks that Lisa is a self-assured young woman who seems mature and sensible. She feels that they will get on well together and that there are not likely to be any problems.

DISCUSSION POINTS

1. What sort of house rules do you think it wise to introduce?

2. How much time are you prepared to spend helping your student settle in happily?

3. How is the family coping with a new person in the home?

6
The Student's Viewpoint

Can you imagine how things might be from the student's point of view? Often it is easy to just not realise how they might be feeling.

BEING AWAY FROM HOME

Leaving home to embark on life as a student is a major change. Everything is new and different. For many, it is their first time of living away from home alone. The sudden freedom from parental restriction can be intoxicating, but some students may feel lonely, homesick and uncertain at first.

Remember your student has to adapt to:

- staying in someone else's home
- living in a different town or even country
- different customs
- being away from their own family and friends
- meeting new people
- a new course of study.

Obviously if the accommodation is comfortable, and the family friendly, this is going to help a great deal. Knowing there is a ready and sympathetic ear available if they have any problems can make all the difference.

THE OVERSEAS STUDENT

Very many overseas students come here to study and experience our way of life. The language school industry is becoming a major one and expanding very rapidly. Some schools appear just for the summer months, others operate all year round. A wide variety of courses are offered to attract the overseas students to our shores. These might include:

I think the English people are the only ones who talk so much about the weather!

English people are in general friendly, but they're sometimes very cold.

The English people is very polite and it's easy to speak with them.

The English make great efforts to make their visitors feel at home.

England is the ideal place for a dog. Everyone has one and everyone loves them. Lucky dogs!

The most surprising thing was that the members of family – even fathers – wash the dishes after dinner every day. It is natural that women should do it in our country.

Fig. 20. What do overseas students think about us?

- academic courses working towards a recognised examination/qualification

- short holiday courses in English combined with visits to places of interest

- sports courses with tuition, for example golf, horse-riding

- business courses

- computer studies

- specialist courses, for example preparation for confirmation classes where students come complete with a priest, take the lessons and then are confirmed when they return home.

Each year new courses become available and the number of students, and subsequently the number of host families, increases.

In addition to language schools, many overseas students come to our universities and colleges to study for degrees, business diplomas and other qualifications. Some are completely fluent and able to study with English students. Others come over and study at international departments on campus.

Coping with culture shock

Britain can seem very strange to those from other countries and there needs to be understanding on both sides. Although the cultural differences may be interesting, exciting and new, they may also be dramatic and adjustment can be difficult. Probably most of us have some prejudices as far as other cultures are concerned, the same as those from other countries have about us. For example, the British are often perceived as a reserved people who love animals and spend a lot of time drinking tea! (See Figure 20.)

A few examples of cultural differences are:

- Some students never say please or thank you. It's not because they are being rude, but rather that there is no equivalent translation in their language.

- Queuing is unknown in some countries, which leads to frequent complaints from people waiting for buses as students push on in front of them.

- In some countries it's against the law to smack your children and a corrective spanking may be interpreted as utter cruelty!

- Nodding and shaking heads can mean no and yes in some countries, instead of the other way around.

- Baths instead of showers are thought unhygienic in some cultures.

- Our homes may be very different from theirs.

- Blowing your nose in front of others could cause offence.

- For men to help with household chores, such as washing up, could mean 'losing face'.

- Women still have a lower status in many countries.

- Having animals in the house, particularly in the kitchen, is disgusting to some students.

- Some students are uncertain about how to address you. Some expect to call you by your first name, others would be very uncomfortable with this as forms of address reflect status. Explain at the beginning what you wish to be called.

Doubtless each host family could contribute quite a few more examples. Talk to your student as much as possible about their traditions and customs, and explain ours carefully.

Getting used to our food

For some reason English food is often not highly thought of abroad. Many landladies will be highly indignant about this, especially as they make great efforts to provide nutritious, balanced meals with plenty of fresh vegetables. Many families are now very health-conscious, avoiding fried foods and cutting down on fats. Ask any foreign student what is different about our food and theirs and they will often be very vague, saying 'It's just *different!*' (See Figure 21).

In this country wives and mothers often work full-time. In many other countries they don't and a lot of time is devoted to cooking. Here, we simply don't have time to spend hours cooking every day and quick, convenience foods may perhaps be used more. Even so, the label that has apparently stuck to our food seems rather unfair. It's a good idea to suggest to your student that they might like to try cooking one day. Give them the chance to show what they enjoy. Usually they will be pleased to do this but check you have the right utensils needed. One Hungarian student made her own pasta for the family and, finding there was nothing to make it into spirals, ingeniously used a cheese grater!

Remember also that many students are actually keen to try our food.

- One student looked in dismay at his cereal and toast and said 'But I thought the English always had a big cooked breakfast with sausage, egg and bacon!'

- An Italian student complained 'Because I am Italian, the family give me spaghetti every day. From a very big tin! I wished very much to have the same as them.'

Try not to get upset if your best English cooking is not appreciated. Be patient and encourage them to try things. Very often they find it is good after all, even if it is different!

Taking differences into account
Remember there are different customs concerning food.

- Some students may leave food on their plates simply as a polite way of showing they have been given plenty, not because it is not liked.

- Certain foods are forbidden in some cultures, for example pork/ham/bacon/sausages to orthodox Muslims or Jews.

- Some students find our times of eating very strange.

- Knives and forks may be held differently.

Packed lunches
Younger students in particular will expect a packed lunch each day they go to school or on a day's outing. Sometimes they will be asked by their teachers what they have to eat and it will be discussed as part of a lesson. Comments from students are carefully noted as part of the school's monitoring of standards. Sadly, not all students receive varied or nutritious food.

Some comments from overseas students about English food

English food is much better than its reputation.

I think it's a little different from other foods but I can't say it's worse than Spanish food.

I don't understand why we have everyday some potatoes. I hate the rice pudding. All the pudding seems strange for me.

English people always have desserts after dinner — sometimes very sweet — and now I am never satisfied unless I have it!!

Early morning tea is a lovely English custom.

English people are very good in tins. They are so lazy in cooking!!

Fig. 21. Comments about English food.

'We get exactly the same every single day – boring jam sandwiches, no drink and never fruit. We usually throw them away and buy a beefburger.' This 13-year-old overseas student was rightly unhappy.

Others in the same class were more than satisfied with what they were given:

'Today I had four sandwiches – two salad and two ham, an individual cheese portion, an apple and an orange drink. I liked everything and it was plenty. I gave one sandwich away to a friend who didn't have much. We don't have the same every day and it's always good.'

Save ice-cream containers and soak the labels off, then use as lunch boxes: cheaper than foil or cling-film, or buying containers.

Speaking English

It's living and speaking regularly with an English family, rather than classroom study, that helps improve the student's command of our language. Time spent in conversation will really be appreciated and is a very important aspect of your student's stay. Evening meal times are especially good for this, when everyone is together and can talk about what happened during the day. Of course mistakes will be made and you should understand:

• Many students are very sensitive and worried about making mistakes.

• They may be afraid that they will not be understood.

• Or they may be afraid they will be laughed at.

Indeed, sometimes things can be amusing and we can't help smiling. One of Judith's student's always very politely addressed her as 'Sir'!

Carol asked a student if she had visited England before and the conversation went like this:

'Yes, last year.'

'Whereabouts did you stay?'

'In Turkey.'

'No – I meant, have you stayed in *England* before?'

'Yes. In Turkey.'

'But Turkey is not in England!'

'Yes, Turkey in England. I show you on map.' Whereupon the student very triumphantly pointed out *Torquay!*

Another student exclaimed about all the sheep on Romney Marsh 'Look at all those *ships*.' Mispronunciations are common but do try to remember your student's feelings. You don't want to discourage them from trying. Give them the chance to teach you a few words of their language and see how you manage some of *their* pronunciation! The English are seen abroad as expecting to be understood wherever they go and usually not bothering, or able, to learn another language.

'What's that barking on the roof?'

'An Englishman trying to learn a foreign language!'

is an overseas joke illustrating this perception.

Respecting students' efforts

Explaining the peculiarities and differences in our language is not always easy. For example, when talking about the time we might say, 'It's ten (or five) past two,' but we don't say 'It's seven past two.' We might instead say it's seven *minutes* past two, or it's nearly ten past. But none of us know why this is! We might say, 'I am going to the cinema, but can you explain why it is wrong for your student to say 'I go to the cinema' when they mean the same thing? Concentrate on everyday English and let the teachers explain the complexities!

Anyone who learns another language, and becomes fluent in it, can only be admired.

ENJOYING STUDENT LIFE

Student life is not just about studying. It is a way of life in itself that many people often look back on with fond memories and sighs of regret that it is over. Often this is the transitional time when fledgling adults fly the nest and try their wings in comparative safety, before venturing out into the hard world of steady jobs and their own family responsibilities.

There is something different to do every evening. There are dozens of different clubs or organisations to join, opportunities for voluntary work – such as running the soup kitchen for the homeless once a week – deep discussions with newly found friends that often go on late into the night, places to visit, the famous students' parties and, of course, inevitable close friendships. Courses may lead to travel opportunities with a year abroad included. The whole experience is there for the student to get as much or as little out of it as they wish.

Making time to study

With so much on offer it is little wonder that studies are sometimes neglected; there almost seems to be not enough time to fit it in. Some students are sensible and dedicated but, with others, frantic late-night sessions are often needed at the last minute to meet deadlines for work to be handed in or to revise for exams. Suddenly it's all go to get things done.

If your student is studying well into the early hours, looks strained and bleary-eyed, don't worry too much or be tempted to offer the benefit of your advice. This is how many of them are and, at the end of the day, organising their studies is their responsibility, not yours.

Getting exam results

Students have a date for their exam results to be put on the notice board. This is the moment of truth, when they find out if their dreams are realised, or whether they are disappointed. Is it to be exhilaration or despair? Telephones are jammed as anxiously waiting families are informed. The day of going for the results can be more nerve-racking than the day of the examination itself. Bear with your student if he seems more than a little on edge at that time!

STUDENT FINANCES

'Being a student means being broke.'

The majority of students at colleges and universities struggle financially. Student grants have been reduced and many families are unable to help out sufficiently. Not only do most students not have much money, they usually haven't had much experience of managing it as effectively as possible. They also have to buy a number of books, which are often very expensive, and this depletes their limited resources still further.

Obviously paying for their board and lodgings should be a priority. An all-in charge which includes accommodation, food, heating, lighting, laundry and so on is helpful in that the student then doesn't have to worry about bills coming in and it makes it easier for them to manage their finances.

In contrast, young overseas summer students often arrive with a great deal of money to spend and they may find things cheaper to buy here than in their own country. But often, because they are young and opportunities are there, they fritter it away. Some youngsters get hooked on amusement arcades and can lose very large amounts.

Because of money difficulties you may sometimes find yourself in the position of either being asked

● to lend money
● or to look after it.

Many people feel it unwise to do either and you may well feel the
same. Students have to take responsibility for their own finances
and, unless there are very exceptional circumstances, it is probably
best not to get involved in this area.

FEELING PART OF THE FAMILY

'My landlady is very pleasant, but she is forever knocking on my
door when I want to be left alone and asking me if I'm OK, if I want
to watch TV, or where I've been when I've been out. Sometimes I
just want to be left alone.'
　'I don't like to sit with the family too much in case I'm intruding.
I hope one of them will knock on my door and ask me if I want to
join them, but they never do. I can't say I feel at home here.'
　Striking the right balance between making your student feel at
home and giving them enough space is sometimes difficult, and a lot
depends on individual personalities and sensitivity.

● Being friendly and showing an interest could be interpreted as
being nosy.

● Trying not to disturb them when they keep to their room can be
mistaken for not wanting them around.

'The family I live with is great. They all spend plenty of time
talking to me and they invite me if they're going out anywhere. They
always smile and make me feel welcome whenever I come into a
room. When I am busy studying they never bother me. I feel able to
relax here.'
　This family has evidently got the balance right! It's not always
easy, but a friendly smile and readiness to listen will create a warmth
to which most students will readily respond.

QUESTIONS AND ANSWERS

*If overseas students are living here in Britain shouldn't they adapt to
our way of doing things?*

Yes, to a point, in that they are here to experience our way of life and must respect our laws and customs. But you cannot expect them to ignore their own values or traditions which have been part of their upbringing and, in turn, you should respect those. For example, certain food may be forbidden, or certain things may cause offence. If there is consideration on both sides and an effort to understand any important differences then problems caused by cultural issues can be kept to a minimum.

I have always expected my children to help with washing and drying up. They feel it very unfair that the students don't help at all. Should students be expected to lend a hand?

If they are living as part of the family then, yes, it is quite reasonable to expect them to at least help clear the table or take a turn at drying up. Some are very good at rushing off as soon as they've finished eating. The majority will help without any prompting. If not, you could always offer a tea-towel and ask 'Would you like to help tonight?'

Do remember though, that with some foreign cultures males are *never* expected to help with such things and they would be horrified to find it was expected!

CHECKLIST

- Be aware that your student has a lot of changes to adapt to.

- Explain our customs and ways of doing things.

- Respect cultural differences even if you do not agree with them.

- Be prepared to spend time talking to your student.

- Make sure you do all you can to make your student feel at home.

CASE STUDIES

Marcus and Sebastian get used to life in England

'This is our first time in England. Everything is different and some things strange. For example, in the bathroom there is a bath but no shower. The rooms have carpets all over the floor – in our houses we have just rugs. We like the food but here we have water to drink with our dinner instead of milk like we do at home. The vegetables are very strange but the puddings are good.

'Everyone takes their shoes off indoors at home. Here people walk into their lounges with shoes on they have worn outside. It's fun talking English every day. We always have very good conversations at meal times. We tried to teach Angela and Tony some of our language but they said it was too difficult to pronounce.'

Lucy finds things difficult

'What is sometimes difficult is that the flat belongs to Claire so she can make the rules. I mean, she can tell me that she wants the lounge to herself because she is having a friend round, but if I want a friend round I can't very well ask her to keep out of her own lounge, can I? Or tell her off for playing music too loudly or not washing up after herself. I think I'm in an awkward position sometimes. It's different when two friends are flat-sharing and splitting the rent. Here it's landlady and lodger. Perhaps if my room was bigger it would make it easier.'

Amanda enjoys the freedom

'I'm an only child and my parents find it hard to accept that now I'm an adult and able to make my own mind up about things. I've never lived away from home before, so coming to university has given me a completely different life and I'm really enjoying it. At first I was nervous and worried that I wouldn't fit in. But it's not like school. Here you are treated as an adult and your opinion is listened to. There's so much to do here – something different every night – clubs and organisations to join and so many interesting people to meet.

'The student grant money doesn't go a long way and I admit that sometimes I have a sandwich instead of a proper meal to save money; most of us do.

'I feel that staying with Helen and Debbie has been a sort of half-way house – away from home but not completely on my own.'

Lisa appreciates her accommodation

'I've stayed in a student bed-sit and in university halls of residence in the past, but living here with Barbara is much more comfortable. I'm very lucky that we get on so well and even the dog makes a fuss of me when I come in! There was no problem at all in settling in. Barbara doesn't have a lot of rules and regulations and she treats me with consideration, which I appreciate. I can study in peace and quiet, invite friends if I want to, or use the lounge when I wish.'

DISCUSSION POINTS

1. How easy has it been to build up a good relationship with your student?

2. Do you feel you could adapt to accommodate cultural differences?

3. What steps could you take to make your student feel part of the family?

7
Troubleshooting

'It's sometimes the smaller things that cause problems. Nothing really serious, but enough to get you annoyed.'

'I've had about fifty students staying with me over the years, but I've only had serious problems with two.'

These sorts of comments are usual. The majority of students are not going to cause you big problems. Of course, you may be unlucky and get one who does and that will obviously be a bad experience. However, most people find that their students are not deliberately troublesome although there may be some minor problems due to not understanding, thoughtlessness, or the sheer intoxication of freedom from parental restraint! Usually these can be sorted out amicably with a quiet, but firm, word.

LOOKING AT SOME COMMON PROBLEMS

You will soon get to know what sort of problems may be most likely to occur and you will be prepared. Forewarned is forearmed.

Not keeping to meal times
It's understandably infuriating if you have cooked the evening meal and your student hasn't come in at the agreed time and hasn't let you know.

- Don't keep everyone else waiting; just start without them.

- If their food is ruined then that's their fault, not yours.

Of course, sometimes there are valid excuses but more often than not it's just that they haven't noticed the time.

Breakfasts are another matter. Many landladies are flexible on this because they know students often don't like getting up in the mornings. One arrangement is to leave it set out but ask them to clear it away and wash up themselves.

Not liking the food

'Mealtimes are my biggest headache. My students don't seem to like any vegetables at all.'

Overseas students especially can sometimes cause considerable problems in this respect. However, remember they are here to experience the British way of life, and this includes trying our food and eating what we eat.

• Put the vegetables in a dish and then they can help themselves or go without as they please.

• Remember they often say they don't like something because they haven't tried it!

• A little side salad is often popular as an alternative to cooked vegetables, and quicker to prepare.

• Although you may want to be a little flexible in providing alternatives this needs to be within reason.

Eating too much

'My students seem hungry all the time. They are always asking for sandwiches in the evenings and a whole bowl of fruit went in one day.'

It's true that some seem to have over-healthy appetites. Others just like eating! Either way you are not expected to supply them with endless food, in excess of normal adequate meals. You might consider an odd sandwich here or there as a late night snack a reasonable request, but either make them yourself or make sure you know what is going in them. Several slices of ham and inch-thick cheese will soon empty your fridge.

When Jenny filled a large bowl high with fruit she expected it to last for most of the week. So to find it empty the very next day was an unexpected shock. True, she had not actually told the students they could only have one or two pieces each every day. But she had wrongly assumed they wouldn't take more. Worse, when she spoke to them about it they admitted they had given some to friends who never had fruit in their house! Jenny told them how she felt about this in no uncertain terms and it didn't happen again.

Coming in late at night

This is one of the most common problems. Students collectively like the night life. If, however, your students are under 16 and haven't come home by 1 or 2 am, when their deadline was 11 pm, you are right to be angry. Some families have sat up, worried out of their minds and longing for their beds, only for the students to come home in the early hours, laughing and quite unconcerned, after having had a good time out. It hasn't entered their heads that anyone would be sitting up waiting for them, wondering if they were safe. In the morning the students have a lie-in but you will probably have to be up early to see to the family. If you have this problem:

- Give your students a firm warning that you will report them to the school next time.

- Be sure to carry out your warning.

- Persistent offenders can be threatened with being sent home. This always works.

Making too much noise

Young people nearly all seem to like noise, which you will have found out if you have teenagers of your own in the house. Some even swear they can't study without music on. Everything has to be at full volume, voices raised and doors slammed. Usually they are quite oblivious to the fact that they may be disturbing you or getting on your nerves so, if they do, tell them. A good-humoured 'Can you turn it down a bit please – I can't hear myself think' is usually enough.

Remember, though, the noise problem works both ways. It could be *you* who is making the noise and interrupting your student's studies! It is often very difficult for a student to ask for quiet in someone else's home.

Bringing friends home

Your permission should always be asked before friends are brought home and you should make this clear at the beginning. If not you may come home, as one host-mother did, to find a huge mound of trainers in the hall and her student happily watching a video with ten friends. Although pleased they had all taken their shoes off she was somewhat taken aback by this invasion. 'They were all well-behaved and not causing any trouble, but that's not the point,' she said, quite rightly. 'I expect to be *asked*!'

Another point is when the student wants a boyfriend/girlfriend to stay overnight. 'We are allowed to at home,' assured one 15-year-old. Tell them straight that they certainly aren't allowed to here! There may, however, well be occasions when you *will* agree to an overnight visitor. If so, you are entitled to make a charge to cover the use of your facilities.

Personal hygiene

Many students come with enough perfumes, sprays, lotions and creams to fill a small suitcase. Sometimes boys have just as much in this line as girls.

On the other hand there are a few who don't seem to know what a deodorant is for. Out of all the possible problems you might encounter, speaking about body odour is the one many people find most difficult to deal with. They are simply too embarrassed to mention it and suffer in silence, rushing around with air fresheners after the student has left the room. It may sound amusing if you haven't experienced this problem, but the reality is very unpleasant and difficult to ignore.

One mother, unable to bring herself to say anything to her student, found her young teenage son less held back by feelings of delicacy. 'What's that pong in here? Someone needs a good bath,' he said bluntly. It worked! Another mother dealt with the situation by buying a deodorant and simply asking if the student would like to try it.

Not having any privacy

It's important that everyone has some privacy, both the family and the student. If, for example, you have someone coming for the evening you want to talk to privately, explain this to your student and ask them to keep out of the way. It's quite reasonable. Ensure too that the student's privacy is respected.

- Always knock and wait for an answer before entering their room.

- Respect any need for solitude and don't let children bother them.

Jealousy within the family

It should be remembered that problems may not come just from the students, but from your own children too. Sometimes children can feel that you are giving too much of your attention to the 'usurpers' and not enough to them. Jealous children can become difficult and bad-mannered, so try to make sure they are not ignored and are made to feel part of everything.

One child had his own method of dealing with foreign students he found tiresome. He 'helped' them with their English but took great delight in teaching them totally incorrect words, much to their embarrassment when they found out later.

Teenagers may feel the students are allowed to do things they aren't, have better clothes or more money, which can lead to feelings of resentment. Be sure you make time to talk these things out.

Using the telephone without permission

You may not know about this until your telephone bill comes in and you have a very nasty shock. It's essential to have an itemised bill so that you can spot unauthorised calls at a glance. Unfortunately, by this time your student may have left and your profit has been seriously eroded.

You can, however, make sure your student is unable to use the phone without your knowledge. If you have a modern digital phone you can have a call-barring system installed, restricting any calls out. You then have a special personal number to use before making a call. You can choose from several different programme options: from restricting all calls except emergency ones, to restricting just long-distance or international ones. British Telecom charges £7 quarterly (inclusive of VAT), but it may well save you more than this and give you peace of mind.

DEALING WITH UNACCEPTABLE BEHAVIOUR

It would not be realistic to think that all problems can be solved by tact, diplomacy and a few well-chosen words. Unfortunately a minority of students will behave in such an unacceptable way that the only method to deal with it is to get them moved. Hopefully this will not happen to you. However, you and your family come first and you cannot be expected to share your home with anyone who does not show respect and behave in a decent manner.

Using bad language

There are some people who frequently use bad language as a matter of course and think nothing of it. You may find this offensive and unacceptable. If so, state firmly that either the language is moderated or the student looks for somewhere else to stay.

Smoking

Smoking is highly unacceptable to many people. You may have asked for a non-smoker and your request overlooked or ignored. If the student cannot agree not to smoke in the house then you should ask for them to be removed as quickly as possible.

Drinking

Many students, even those who are normally responsible, may come home occasionally a little the worse for drink. There are on-going parties and it's easy to have the odd lapse and drink too much. However, it is another matter entirely when the drinking gets out of hand and becomes seriously heavy and frequent. A student who is brought home practically insensible and throws up on your carpet, or who falls up the stairs singing loudly, is no joke and you do not have to tolerate this sort of thing. Once is more than enough. Some landladies will give a severe warning, others will not risk it happening again and will see that the student is moved.

If you have under-age students and find they have been drinking you have a responsibility to contact the student leader or accommodation officer right away. They will take a very serious view of the matter and deal with it appropriately.

Taking illegal drugs

This is one of the biggest worries. Certainly these drugs are easily available to many students but this doesn't mean that they all take them. Indeed many of them are very much anti-drugs. However, it's a fact that some students do take drugs and you may be worried yours is one of them. Some will take them simply because they are there to be taken and their friends are taking them. Others may want to blot out problems or exam pressures, or they may feel lonely or unhappy. It may be just a passing experimental phase, or become a serious problem. Younger students away from the parental eye for the first time are particularly vulnerable.

Some of the signs to watch for are:

- sudden changes of mood from happy and alert to sullen and moody
- unusual irritability or aggression
- loss of appetite
- loss of interest in things generally
- bouts of drowsiness or sleepiness
- telling lies or furtive behaviour
- loss of money from the house

- unusual smells, stains or marks on the body, clothes or around the house
- unusual powders, tablets, scorched tinfoil, needles or syringes.

It's not always easy to tell when someone is on drugs as some of the signs, such as mood swings, are the same as those of normal adolescence. They could be drowsy or sleepy simply because they've had a lot of late nights or have been studying into the early hours. So it's important not to panic and jump to conclusions. You can only be sensible and vigilant. If you do have cause for suspicion do talk to someone from the student's organisation as quickly as possible. There are also drug advice helplines (see Useful Addresses) which are available 24-hours a day.

Remember that, although there is a great deal of publicity about drug-taking in the media, there are plenty of sensible young people around who have never touched drugs and are never likely to.

Theft

It is very sad when you welcome someone into your home to find you are repaid by having something stolen. Some landladies only find out after the student has left that a favourite CD or tape has disappeared. Others may have the very unpleasant experience of finding all their housekeeping money has been taken. Keep cash in the house to a minimum. Make sure your handbag is not left lying about and have a lockable drawer or small safe for bank books, credit cards and jewellery. Do not keep your cheque book with your cheque card.

- Do make sure you have your facts right before you make any accusations. Be certain that you have not simply misplaced something.

- Do insist that organisations remove any student caught stealing immediately.

WHAT TO DO ABOUT DAMAGE

Damage to your property or possessions is both annoying and upsetting. The first thing to establish is whether it is

a) accidental, or

b) deliberate vandalism

Hopefully your student will tell you if they have broken anything and offer to pay for it, but this is not always the case. Sometimes a student could be worried about what you might say, so will keep quiet and hope you won't find out.

Example

- It took three days for Maria to pluck up courage to say the leg of her bed had broken as she got into it, because she feared she would be blamed. Meanwhile, she slept uncomfortably on the floor. The host family were horrified – not about the bed but because she had slept on the floor! The broken bed leg was clearly seen as their responsibility.

- Another student broke the window in his room. He did not say anything to the landlady because he thought he would be expected to pay for it and was broke. The problem was made worse because this was in the winter and the room became freezing with wind and rain blowing in. When the landlady found out she was rightly angry because broken windows obviously should be repaired immediately or at least boarded up against the weather. The student was suitably ashamed and reimbursed the landlady for the cost of repair when he was able to afford it.

Deliberate damage is another matter, as the wardrobe covered in long deep knife scratches discovered on the student's last day. Episodes such as this are thankfully rare. It is important to contact the school immediately and ask for help. You may or may not get it. Unfortunately some schools will just shrug and say it's your problem to sort out. Others will help you claim reimbursement from the student, or their parents, and this is sometimes successful. It's more difficult if the culprit is an overseas student who has left the country, but a written appeal to the parents with an estimate for the repair or replacement can work, particularly if it's backed up with a report from the school. Failing that, check on your household insurance to see if you can make a claim.

ACCIDENTS AND ILLNESS

Hopefully everyone in the home, family and students, will remain well or with nothing more than a slight cold. However, accidents and illness strike when least expected.

Seeing the doctor

Universities and some colleges will have their own doctor on campus for students to see when necessary. Otherwise, students have the right to consult your doctor as temporary residents. They will be asked to complete a short form. Some students, especially younger overseas ones, may ask you to go with them.

Finding a dentist

Some establishments have an arrangement with a local dental practice for their students. If your own dentist is unable to see your student then it is a matter of phoning around to find one. Dental charges can be expensive. Students from overseas usually have some kind of medical insurance so that they can claim back the cost of any treatment.

Students being admitted to hospital

It's very unfortunate if your student has to be admitted to hospital and perhaps needs an operation, but it happens. Most students are far from their families, and can be without many visitors, which makes the whole experience even worse. However, hospital voluntary help organisers are often wonderful in helping here. They have an army of willing volunteers and have sometimes been able to produce, in the case of a hospitalised foreign student, a volunteer of the same nationality to chat with them.

Being ill yourself

Should you unfortunately fall ill yourself, you may find that you are unable to continue the arrangement of looking after your student. If this happens make sure the organisation concerned is contacted as quickly as possible. They will have emergency accommodation provision if you have to ask for the student to be moved.

If it's just a minor ailment where a day or two in bed will do the trick, make sure the rest of the family lend a hand so that you can rest and regain your strength. It won't hurt them, or the student, to prepare their own meals!

STAYING IN CONTROL

It's important to be:

- firm
- fair
- and consistent

about things right from the start. There are some students who will practically make a takeover bid if they are allowed to and who think they can do what they like. You have to make quite clear that this is your home and while in it they must respect your wishes. The primary rule is: *deal with any problem immediately* because:

• If your student does something you find unacceptable, and you don't speak up about it, they are likely to do it again.

• The longer you leave unsatisfactory matters, the more difficult they will become to resolve.

• The student needs to understand it's you who makes the rules.

• Don't be tempted to ignore things you aren't happy about and hope they will go away. They rarely will and could result in a minor problem becoming a major one.

• Do stand firm and insist a student is removed if this is what you want.

• Don't let one bad experience put you off having more students.

QUESTIONS AND ANSWERS

My student is at university. What do I say if her parents phone up and ask how she is when I know she's neglecting her studies, living it up until the early hours and drinking too much?

This can be a difficult one. Students who are legally adults will not thank you for involving their parents, especially if they are only having a temporary fling before settling down to serious studying. They may well – and perhaps rightly – think it is none of your business. On the other hand, if you are a parent yourself you may not be able to ignore serious concerns and feel you have to say something. If you are directly asked, you are in an awkward position. You can only trust your instincts to do what you think is best, dependent on your level of concern. However, you should speak to your student first about how you feel and warn her of what you might say.

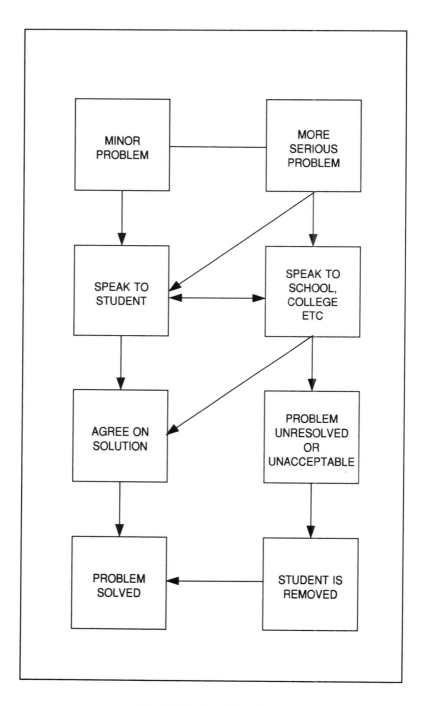

Fig. 22. Problem flowchart.

I have foreign students who speak very limited English and our problem is one of communication. They often don't understand what I am trying to ask them and conversation is impossible. What's the answer?

If you are having foreign students then you must expect some communication difficulties! The main things you need here are patience and a sense of humour. Many students are so nervous of making mistakes that they hardly speak at all to begin with. Encourage them to talk whenever you can. Explain things slowly, in simple terms, accompanied by plenty of 'showing' actions. Sign language can be understood the world over! If there is an important issue you are not getting through on, try writing it down – often students understand written English more easily than spoken.

What should I do I if don't get paid on time?

Reputable organisations will usually pay your money on the dot. It has been known for payments from some organisations to be late and need chasing up, but this seems to be rare.

Where students are responsible for making their own payments there is occasionally a problem when the student has 'forgotten' to pay or has mismanaged his money because he is not used to budgeting. If your money hasn't been offered on the agreed date ask for it and be firm. Do not allow arrears to mount up. Ask the college or university accommodation officer for help or advice if you need to. Usually they will make suggestions, but prefer the matter to be resolved between the two of you. However, in serious cases the establishment concerned will sometimes help by threatening to hold back the student's certificate or award until any arrears are paid.

CHECKLIST

- Speak to your student quickly if you are not happy about anything.

- Try to resolve matters between you.

- If you are unable to sort things out or the problem is serious, ask for help from the school or college.

- If matters cannot be resolved to your satisfaction insist the student is moved.

- If appropriate ask the police for help or advice.

- Stay in control.

CASE STUDIES

Marcus and Sebastian stay out late

Marcus and Sebastian were usually in around 10.30 pm, which was the time specified by the language school. However, one evening they did not come home on time and as it grew later Angela became increasingly concerned. Marcus and Sebastian eventually turned up at nearly 1 am. They had been enjoying themselves at a beach-party. The boys expected Angela and Tony to have gone to bed and that they could sneak in quietly. They were not prepared for Angela to be waiting up.

Angela told them exactly how she felt. Not only had she been worried about their safety, she was extremely tired and also angry. She warned them that it had better not happen again. Marcus and Sebastian had the grace to look ashamed and apologised.

Tony backed Angela by speaking to them the next day. He said he knew they were on holiday and wanted to have a good time but that it wasn't fair to make Angela worry. It was agreed that on Fridays and Saturdays, if there was a special party, they could occasionally be allowed to stay out a little later than the recommended time if this was arranged in advance.

It's Lucy who has the problems

As Lucy worked shift hours, she sometimes went several days without seeing much of Claire. If she was on an early shift Lucy was always careful to be quiet so as not to disturb Claire. However, Claire unfortunately did not show the same consideration to Lucy when Lucy was trying to sleep in the day after being on night duty. She played her CDs at top volume and did not even shut the lounge door, which would have helped a little.

Also, Claire and Lucy had agreed to share basics like milk, tea, coffee and bread, and had a kitty for this which either could take from to replace these items as they were used. However, Lucy was constantly finding there was no milk left for her breakfast cereal, and once no money in the kitty either although she had put her agreed share in. 'Oh, I'm sorry, I had to borrow it,' Claire apologised, 'you don't mind having just toast today do you?'

Lucy did mind, and understandably got annoyed about these

things, but felt she was in a difficult situation. She thought if she complained Claire might ask her to leave. At the same time she thought Claire was being rather thoughtless. Lucy decided that if she had to spend extra to buy items she had already put money in the kitty for she would deduct the amount next time.

Helen is worried about Amanda

Helen did not see a great deal of Amanda since she was out until late most evenings. Having over-protective parents, now that she was away from them Amanda was making sure she enjoyed all that university life had to offer and the company of new friends.

When Amanda was in one weekend, Helen noticed she looked tired and unwell. She tried talking to her but Amanda said she was fine. She often skipped breakfast and although she said she was 'eating with friends' in the evenings Helen suspected she was not having an adequate diet. Worries went through her mind that Amanda could be anorexic or even on drugs and she resolved to keep a close eye on her.

Lisa has an accident

When Lisa went off to play tennis in the park one afternoon nobody expected that it would end with her being taken off to hospital by ambulance. She had the misfortune to tear her Achilles tendon and had fallen to the ground in extreme pain.

Lisa's tennis partner came to tell Barbara, and to collect Lisa's toiletries and nightwear. The accident resulted in an operation for Lisa and a plaster being put on her leg.

When Barbara went to visit her in hospital she found Lisa despondent, thinking that her teacher-training course, which was so important to her, would now have to be postponed. Although she felt well in herself how was she going to manage with a leg in plaster?

Barbara said she thought they could work something out. Luckily there were no steps in the bungalow to worry about. They could borrow a folding wheelchair from the local branch of the Red Cross, and Barbara offered to drive Lisa to college each day when she felt able to return and to pick her up. Hopefully Lisa would not need to miss too much and, at college, with crutches and help from friends, she would be able to manage. Although Lisa would have to spend some time completing teaching practice at a local school she would be out of plaster by then.

DISCUSSION POINTS

1. How tolerant are you prepared to be with student misdemeanours?

2. What sort of problems would you feel unable to cope with?

3. What steps could you take to avoid some problems happening in the first place?

8
Saying Goodbye

The course will inevitably come to an end and your student will prepare to move out. You may breathe a sigh of relief or feel a bit sad as you wave them off, depending on how things have gone. Hopefully, though, it has been a positive and beneficial experience and you will want to do it again.

PACKING AND LEAVING ARRANGEMENTS

Don't expect your student to spend the last night at home with the family – few do! Usually the last night is party night. There will be end-of-course celebrations, saying goodbye to friends, and plenty of excitement, tears and laughter. They've had a good time, done lots of new things and now it's all come to an end.

If your student is leaving with a group by coach, make sure you know what time he needs to be there. Make sure he knows too! You will need to check with the younger ones that their cases are ready and packed in plenty of time. A large number leave things to literally half-an-hour before they are due to leave and then get in a panic because they can't fit everything in. Or they rush to the shops for some last minute bits and pieces and are so late getting back that you start worrying that they will miss the coach.

Last-minute check
Before they leave, check and make sure:

• Nothing has been left in any of the drawers or cupboards.

• All the items which should be in the room are still there.

• There is nothing broken or damaged.

• Your key is handed back.

113

How students enjoyed their stay

I appreciate the open atmosphere in discussions. courses and materials in the fields of science. education and spirituality.

When I go back to my country I'm going to miss my new friends. We've done so many good things together.

Staying with an English family makes the visit to England more interesting.

England is a special country with an interesting culture.

I will never forget this stay: you are all very kind. I will keep a good memory and thank you for having made this stay wonderful.

Fig. 23. How students enjoyed their stay.

KEEPING IN TOUCH

Many students and families enthusiastically promise to keep in touch and may mean it at the time. However, don't expect too much. A few do write regularly to each other for many years, but they are the exception. It takes two to keep up a correspondence and, in most cases, it is likely to inevitably slow down and probably stop. Everyone has their own lives to lead, with many new and increasing demands on their time. Letter-writing, for the majority, is unfortunately something which gets put to one side and often forgotten. Perhaps just exchanging cards and letters at Christmas is more realistic.

Staying with the student's family

Some host families who have got on with their student particularly well have received an invitation to visit their student's family abroad, which is a wonderful opportunity. Joyce and her husband accepted an invitation to visit their student's family home in Italy: 'We were looked after extremely well. They gave us a fantastic holiday. We saw so much more than we could have done as ordinary tourists and it was an unforgettable experience.'

Living with the natives of a country is certainly the best way to really find out about it and see what life is like there, just as the overseas students do when they come over here.

HAVING THE HOUSE TO YOURSELVES AGAIN

Once your student has gone the house may seem strangely quiet and empty. Make the most of the peace! However well you have got on together it's good to have the house to yourselves again and have a break from the extra work that looking after an additional person entails.

If it's the end of the academic year or summer student season, you may have a few months' rest from having students. If you plan to have both kinds of students and take them in all the year round, it's a good idea to arrange at least a short break. Make the most of this in-between time to:

- relax and have more time for yourself and the family
- take a holiday
- go away to visit friends or relatives
- have friends or relatives to stay
- carry out any necessary repairs or decorating in the house.

Having a break and a change will mean you are fresh and rested before having to get used to your next student.

Giving yourself a treat

Make sure you indulge yourself a little. The extra income you've received is because *you* have earned it, so you deserve to feel some personal benefit from it. Maybe it's a holiday, new clothes or some item you've always wanted. Or maybe it's just time to yourself without having to worry about providing a meal at a fixed time. Whatever it is – treat yourself!

EVALUATING YOUR EXPERIENCES

- 'The students are like a breath of fresh air. They have so much enthusiasm for life, so much to talk about, so many interests.'

- 'They keep me young, that's why I like them around.'

- 'Without having students we could never have afforded to go on holiday. The extra money we made paid for that and we had a wonderful time.'

- 'I wish I had known more about what to expect in advance. At least now I'm well prepared for next time.'

- 'With my own children grown up and left home I enjoyed the company of the students.'

These were some of the answers families gave when asked to comment on their experiences with accommodating students. Now that your first student season, or term, is over look back and consider how it went.

- Was it all worth it?

- Did all go as you had hoped?

- Do you have some good memories?

- Did you get something more than just extra income?

Many people, and hopefully you among them, will give a very

positive 'yes' to all these questions. You will also have gained experience of what to expect for the next time.

PLANNING FOR THE FUTURE

After your first student season or term you will decide whether or not you want to carry on next year. Many families or landladies are quite happy to carry on year in and year out and it becomes very much a way of life for them. You may want to do exactly the same, or you may want to try a different organisation or type of student. Take another look around to see what else might be available.

You may even feel that having students is the first step to your own bed and breakfast business, or to running a small guest house. It gives you the experience of dealing with different kinds of people and providing them with a similar type of service. Often one thing leads to another.

- 'Each year when I go on holiday I am very observant of what is provided in the guest house or hotel and compare it with what I offer my students. I often think the students get a much better service for half the cost! Because I enjoy having visitors, and live in an area which has lots of tourists, I often think I might run my own small guest house business one day.'

QUESTIONS AND ANSWERS

Will I have to apply again to the organisation next year or will I automatically be offered another student?

Usually your details will be kept on a database and you will be asked to complete a new application form each year which should be sent out to you well in advance. All registers need to be kept up to date, and it's possible your circumstances will have changed and some of your details will need amending.

My student has a younger sister who would like to come on a summer language school course next year. Is it possible to arrange that she is allocated to stay with me?

Requests like this are sometimes made and usually language schools will do their best to arrange it. When the course place is booked there is usually the opportunity for the student to indicate any specific accommodation requirements. She can then request that she stays with a particular registered host family – yours – and should ensure this is clearly shown on her booking form. Her request should then be passed on to your local language school accommodation office, who should in turn check with you. However, do remember there are often thousands of bookings to be dealt with by an extremely busy office, so any particular requests like this should be made as early as possible.

CHECKLIST

* Make sure you know what time the student's transport is going to leave.

* Check that the packing has been done.

* Look in all the drawers and cupboards to see that nothing has been left behind.

* Check that everything which should be in the room is still there.

* Give yourself a special treat.

* Think over how everything went.

* Make plans for the next student.

CASE STUDIES

Angela and Tony feel things went well

Angela and Tony were glad that they had decided to have two students at a time. Angela felt that with young teenagers it was good that they had each other for company, especially when coming home at night, and that having two did not really mean much more work than just one.

During the first season they had overseas students for eight weeks. After Marcus and Sebastian left Anna and Maria came for two weeks, then two more girls for three weeks. The most difficult part, Angela found, was providing a balanced menu that they all liked and which satisfied healthy teenage appetites. She found that her own children seemed to enjoy having the students to stay and that the students all spent some time playing with them.

As soon as each payment cheque was received and banked Angela would transfer half the amount into a savings account to build into a little nest egg. The other half covered the costs of providing for the students and also boosted the general family budget, allowing for a few little extras.

'I think eight weeks was long enough,' said Angela, 'but overall I enjoyed it and found the extra money made it well worth doing. We will certainly do it again next year.'

Claire found things were not so easy as she had imagined

Claire admitted that sharing her flat with Lucy was not quite as easy as she had imagined. They had not become friends, and had very different personalities and outlooks.

'I found that sometimes she was in the way. There were times when I brought a friend home and Lucy would be in the lounge watching TV when we wanted to be alone. And other times she made me feel guilty for playing CDs when she was trying to sleep.'

Lucy felt that Claire was only interested in the extra income and was not prepared to put herself out in the least. 'I did my best to be a good and considerate lodger but I don't feel Claire was a good landlady. She didn't provide any heating for my room and she didn't seem to like it when I was in the lounge, even though she had told me I could use it. Really I think I made a mistake moving in. I know it's Claire's flat but if she wants someone to share it she should be be more prepared to make them comfortable.'

Lucy only stayed two months with Claire. After that she moved out to share a flat with two other student nurses, where she had a larger room to herself.

Helen though it was worth it in spite of the worry

Helen felt that Amanda had not made much extra work for her. She looked after her own room, got her own breakfast and did her own laundry. Helen found the extra income made a noticeable difference, and put this into a special fund towards a much dreamed of summer holiday abroad which she was able to go ahead and book. This was the positive side of things.

However, Helen found that, as a mother of a teenage girl herself, she had been unable to help worrying about Amanda even though she was officially an adult and not Helen's responsibility.

'I knew it was the first time Amanda had been away from home and her parents are the rather over-protective type. I suppose it was natural that the freedom of student life went to her head at first. I felt she wanted to try every new experience going, which did worry me considerably and I could have done without that! However, it's difficult when someone is living in your home to remain uninvolved and not worry, at least that's what I found. Luckily she did settle down to work eventually.'

Amanda was at university for three years. She stayed with Helen for the first year, moving out to share a student house with friends after that. After Amanda left Helen decided to go ahead and registered with the university for another student.

Barbara and Lisa promise to keep in touch

Barbara found that she was really upset when it was time for Lisa to go. They had got on so well together, having many long and interesting conversations. Lisa had been very appreciative of Barbara's help after her accident, and Barbara had enjoyed having someone to fuss over. For Barbara, although the extra income was welcome, the companionship had been the most important aspect.

'I was really lucky to have someone like Lisa. She has been a pleasure to have here and I'm going to miss her a lot. She has such a lively mind and we've had many stimulating debates on all sorts of topics. I think she will be an excellent teacher and I hope we stay in touch.'

Lisa found Barbara was like a second mother. 'She was always ready with a listening ear and was so easy to talk to. She would give me the benefit of her opinion if asked for but, at the same time, never tried to interfere in anything and always allowed me all the privacy I wanted. I felt at home here right from the beginning. After my accident Barbara was marvellous – I couldn't have coped without her. Certainly we're going to keep in touch and I'm going to introduce her to my mum – they'd get on really well!'

DISCUSSION POINTS

1. How would your experiences help you with any future students?

2. What were the advantages to the family?

3. What aspects of taking in a student have you most enjoyed?

Glossary

Academic year. University/college/school study year, usually starting in September or October and finishing in June or July.

Accommodation officer. Employee of a college or university who liaises between students and providers of accommodation.

ARELS. Association of Recognised English Language Services.

BASELT. British Association of State English Language Teaching.

Bed and breakfast. Accommodation and breakfast are provided.

Board and lodging charge. A fee which includes an amount for both accommodation and food.

British Council. Promotes cultural, educational and technical cooperation between Britain and other countries.

Campus. The grounds and buildings of a university or college.

Cash flow. Movement of money in and out of an account.

Charge advice service. Telephone service for pricing phone calls.

Code of practice. A set of principles/points of guidance to be followed to ensure a certain standard.

Culture shock. The experience of suddenly encountering different customs and lifestyles.

Emergency stand-by. Providing last-minute accommodation.

Full board. Accommodation and all meals are provided.

Half-board. Accommodation, breakfast and evening meal are provided.

Halls of residence. Residential buildings offering student accommodation in a university.

Homestay/host family accommodation. Where the student lives with a family and is treated as a member of it.

Inventory. A detailed list of items in the room you are letting.

On spec. Informal expression meaning as a speculation, or gamble, on the off-chance.

Options. Different choices which are available.

Referee. A person willing to testify to the character or capabilities of your potential tenant.

Reference request. A letter to a referee asking them to provide details about your student.

Rent a Room scheme. A tax-allowance scheme to encourage the letting of rooms in homes.

Reverse charge call. Telephone service obtainable through the operator.

TEFL qualification. Teaching English as a Foreign Language certificate.

Verbal agreement. An agreement which is spoken rather than written.

Vetting visits. A visit which is specifically to inspect and check accommodation and families for suitability.

Vocational course. A course for a particular profession or trade.

Further Reading

FREE BOOKLETS

Rooms to Let, Including the Rent a Room scheme, Personal Taxpayer Series IR87 (Inland Revenue). Available from your tax office.

Letting Rooms in Your Home, Housing Booklet Number 22 (Department of the Environment). Available from Citizens' Advice Bureaux.

Feeling at Home, A guide to cultural issues for those involved in the housing of overseas students (The British Council). Available from some language schools.

Your Practical Guide to Crime Prevention (Home Office Public Relations Branch). Available from your local police station.

Beat the Burglar, Make your home more secure (Home Office Public Relations Branch). Available from your local police station.

Your Home Fire Safety Guide, Pages of advice from Britain's Fire Brigades (Home Departments and Central Office of Information). Available from your local fire station.

Drugs, A Parent's Guide. The signs, the dangers, what to do (Department of Health). Available from Health Promotion Units.

BOOKS

How to Survive at College, David Acres (How To Books, 1987).

How to Study and Live in Britain, Jane Woolfenden (How To Books, 1990).

How to Start a Business from Home, Graham Jones (How To Books, 1994).

Managing Your Personal Finances, John Claxton (How To Books, 1996).

Useful Addresses

The Association of Recognised English Language Services (ARELS), 2 Pontypool Place, Valentine Place, London SE1 8QF. Tel: (0171) 242 3136.

The British Association of State English Language Teaching, BASELT Secretariat, Cheltenham and Gloucester College of Higher Education, Francis Close Hall, Swindon Road, Cheltenham, Gloucestershire GL50 4AZ. Tel: (01242) 227099.

The British Council, Medlock Street, Manchester M15 4AA. Tel: (0161) 9577000.

The British Council, 1 Beaumont Place, Oxford OX1 2PJ. Tel: (01865) 57236.

The British Refugee Council, Bondway House, 3/9 Bondway, London SW8 1SJ. Tel: (0171) 582 6922. (Advice to refugees in Britain, open 9.45am–12.45pm, Mon, Tues, Thurs, Fri, appointments necessary.)

Department for Education and Employment, Sanctuary Buildings, Great Smith Street, Westminster, London SW1P 3BT. Tel: (0171) 925 5000.

Department for Education and Employment for Northern Ireland, Rathgael House, Balloo Road, Bangor, Co. Down BT19 2PR. Tel: (01247) 279000.

Health Publications Unit, Heywood Stores, No 2 Site, Manchester Road, Heywood, Lancashire OL10 2PZ. Tel: (0800) 555777.

The Home Office, Immigration and Nationality Department, Lunar House, Wellesley Road, Croydon CR9 2BY. Tel: (0181) 686 0688. (Open 8.30am–4pm, Mon–Fri.)

Local public enquiry offices:

Belfast: Olive Tree House, Fountain Street, Belfast. Tel: (01232) 322547. (Open 2pm–4.30pm, Tues–Thurs.)

Birmingham: Birmingham Airport. Tel: (0121) 6067345. (Open 9.30am–3pm, Mon–Fri).

Glasgow: Admin Block D, Glasgow Airpor¹ Glasgow. Tel: (0141) 8872255. (Open 9.30am – 12.30pm and 2pm – 4pm, Mon-Fri.)
Harwich: Immigration Office, Parkeston Quay, Harwich. Tel: (01255) 504371. (Open 2pm–4.30pm Mon–Sun.)
Liverpool: Immigration Office, Graeme House, Derby Square, Liverpool. Tel: (0151) 2368974. (Open 2pm–4pm, Tues–Fri.)
Norwich: Immigration Office, Norwich Airport, Norwich. Tel: (01603) 408859. (Open 2.30pm–5pm, Mon–Fri.)
Joint Council for the Welfare of Immigrants, 115 Old Street, London EC1V 9JT. Tel: (0171) 251 8706. (Advice on nationality, immigration and general welfare. Telephone for an appointment.)
National Bureau for Students with Disabilities, 336 Brixton Road, London SW9 7AA. Tel: (0171) 274 0565.
The National Union of Students (NUS), 461 Holloway Road, London N7 6LJ. Tel: (0171) 272 8900. (Information and practical help, welfare issues and students' rights.)
The National Union of Students (Northern Ireland), 29 Bedford Street, Belfast BT2 7EJ. Tel: (01232) 244641.
The National Union of Students (Scotland), 11 Broughton Market, Edinburgh EH3 7NU. Tel: (0131) 556 6598.
SCODA (the Standing Conference on Drug Abuse), 1 Hatton Place, London EC1 8ND. Tel: (0171) 430 2341.
Scottish Education Department, Haymarket House, Clifton Terrace, Edinburgh EH12 5DT. Tel: (0131) 556 8400.
United Kingdom Council for Overseas Student Affairs (UKCOSA), 60 Westbourne Grove, London W2 5SH. Tel: (0171) 229 9268.
United Kingdom Immigrants Advisory Service (UKIAS), 190 Great Dover Street, London SE1 4YB. Tel: (0171) 357 6917. (Advice and practical help with immigration problems.)
UKIAS Refugee Unit (address as UKIAS). Tel: (0171) 357 7421.

Index

CASH FROM YOUR COMPUTER
How to sell word processing, book-keeping, desktop publishing and other services

Zoe King

As a computer owner, you know that you use your computer to just a fraction of its real capacity. Now, with the help of this book, you can capitalise on a major asset which spends most of its time sitting idly on your desk. This book tells you everything you need to know about selling your services in the fields of word processing, desktop publishing, book-keeping, and a great deal more. You'll find advice on unusual sources of extra income, as well as help in choosing the most appropriate and cost-effective software and hardware. Here at last is a computer user's book which will help you take advantage of *all* the money-making potentials open to you. Zoe King was until recently the Sales and Marketing Director of a computer software company. She is a freelance writer and editor, who has for several years supplemented her income by offering computer services to local companies, charities, and individuals.

£8.99 160pp illus. 1 85703 338 8.

WINNING CONSUMER COMPETITIONS
How to scoop valuable cash and other prizes time and time again

Kathy Kantypowicz

The definitive guide to winning competitions, this volume will show you how you too can stake your claim to some of the millions of glittering prizes offered to consumers every year. Learn how to find entry forms, research your answers and, most important of all, write those few well chosen tie-breaker words which can scoop cars, family holidays, household appliances, clothing, TV and hi-fi equipment, cash and almost any other luxury item you care to name. Why buy when you can win? This book may revolutionise your shopping habits forever. It's easy and it's fun to be a winner! Kathy Kantypowicz has won more than £200,000 worth of prizes and is dubbed 'The Queen of Competitions' by the British Press. Now editor of *Competitors World* magazine, she was formerly resident competition expert on *The Big Breakfast Show* and has appeared regularly in television, press and radio features.

£8.99, 160pp. illus. 1 85703 333 7.